TALKING LIFE

TALKING
LIFE

JAVED AKHTAR

IN CONVERSATION WITH
NASREEN
MUNNI KABIR

WESTLAND
NON·FICTION

First published by Westland Non-Fiction, an imprint of Westland Books, a division of Nasadiya Technologies Private Limited, in 2023

No. 269/2B, First Floor, 'Irai Arul', Vimalraj Street, Nethaji Nagar, Allappakkam Main Road, Maduravoyal, Chennai 600095

Westland, the Westland logo, Westland Non-Fiction and the Westland Non-Fiction logo are the trademarks of Nasadiya Technologies Private Limited, or its affiliates.

ISBN: 9789395767668

10 9 8 7 6 5 4 3 2 1

Typeset by SÜRYA, New Delhi

Printed at Parksons Graphics Pvt. Ltd

To life, the most unpredictable beloved.

– Javed Akhtar

TALKING LIFE

NMK: How does one define a good life? And would you say your life has turned out the way you had wanted it to?

JA: As a young man, I could never have imagined the shape my life would take. I've been through many experiences, lived in many cities and houses, met so many people in such different circumstances—it has been a life of dramatic twists and turns with some good and bad moments. I suppose if I could've guessed early on what might happen to me, there'd be no excitement to look forward to. It's like knowing the end of a film before the first scene starts.

NMK: So much has happened in your life that it's difficult to know where we should start. The first time we sat down to talk resulted in the 1999 book *Talking Films* and then in 2002, we spoke at length about lyrics in *Talking Songs*. This third book in our trilogy aims to look at your life. I suppose it's best not to be too clever and just start at the beginning.

JA: Let's start with my paternal great-great-grandfather, Fazl-e-Imam, who was the Sadr-us Sudur [Chief Justice] in Delhi. His son, Allama Fazl-e-Haq Khairabadi, was a distinguished scholar, philosopher and poet. He edited the *Diwan-e-Ghalib* on Ghalib's request and, at one time, he too was a Chief Justice in the State of Awadh. In later years, Allama Fazl-e-Haq became a freedom fighter and joined the council of twenty-one members who were organising the 1857 revolt against the British. Being a man of law, he was asked to write the Constitution of Azad Hindustan, in which he had suggested capital punishment for cow slaughter. The prominent journalist Balbir Punj, an ex-BJP MP who was in the Rajya Sabha, wrote about this.

Allama Fazl-e-Haq was arrested for inciting people to take part in the 1857 revolt and was jailed by the British in a colonial prison in the Andaman Islands, which is still known as Kala Pani [Black Waters]. He died there in exile in 1861. Orders were passed to have Fazl-e-Haq's house demolished and the Raja Sahib of Kamlapur, Khairabad, who was a proud Thakur, asked if he could buy the debris of my great-grandfather's home. He managed to buy it from the British and had the debris transported to the Raja's own vast estate where it was preserved. I managed to find the original demolition orders—they are still with me—it's a piece of history.

Allama Fazl-e Haq's son, Abdul Haq, was also a renowned scholar. He ran a madrasa—by madrasa I do not mean some madrasas talked about these days; these were real schools of knowledge. He used to tell his students, 'If freedom comes after I die, you must come to my grave and let me know that India has become independent.' Abdul Haq died in 1897 and exactly fifty years later, in 1947, India became independent.

Some of Abdul Haq's students still lived in the town, though they were old men by 1947, but one of them remembered his teacher's words. So, this elderly gentleman started walking slowly towards the cemetery where Abdul Haq was buried. As he passed through the town, other people came to know the story and joined him. Soon, a huge procession formed and stood by their teacher's grave, while his old student said:

Abdul Haq Sahib, Hindustan azaad ho gaya. [Abdul Haq Sahib, India is free]

Mithai was then distributed among those present in the graveyard. This is a real incident.

Our family has private burial plots in a Khairabad cemetery where five or six generations have been buried—aunts, uncles, grandparents and great-grandparents. I went to the graveyard some years ago and took some photographs. Now, the gates are locked and no one else can be buried there.

NMK: Can we speak about your famous grandfather, Muztar Khairabadi. How was he related to Abdul Haq?

JA: Abdul Haq's sister, Syedunnisan Hirmaan, was Muztar's mother. She wrote poetry in an era when only courtesans were allowed to, while girls of good families were not supposed to. Most of her work is now lost and only a few of her poems can be found in selected anthologies. Initially, she was the person who corrected her son's poetry. Not just proofreading, it was correcting. 'Don't use that word, use this.' It is called islah [to improve, to better].

A famous poet in his era, Muztar Khairabadi, was born in 1865. He was celebrated for his ghazals, dohas, thumris and bhajans. Several of Muztar's couplets are very popular though many people today are unaware that they were written by him. For example:

Waqt do mujh par kathin guzre hain saari umr mein
Ik tere aane se pehle ik tere jaane ke baad
[Two instances in my life have been hard to bear, the first before you came, the second after you left.]

The first line of another famous ghazal by Muztar goes:

Na kisi ki aankh ka noor hoon na kisi ke dil ka qaraar hoon
[I am neither the light of someone's eyes, nor the tranquillity of someone's heart.]

This ghazal was mistakenly believed to have been written by Bahadur Shah Zafar, but in fact it was by Muztar. All the current

historians and scholars of Urdu literature have confirmed this. More
details of this ghazal can be found in the book *Gulshan,* which has
a selection of Muztar's poems and is published by Rekhta. Muztar's
famous malhar ('Chha rahi oodi ghata jiyra mora ghabaraaye hai'
[Purple clouds fill the sky, uneasiness fills my heart] has been sung by
the celebrated singer Begum Akhtar. Muztar has also written several
dohas on Lord Krishna. Many of his dohas are on the Rekhta website.

Like his forefathers, my grandfather was also a judge. I have heard
many stories about him. He was a well-to-do man and played the
sitar and harmonium and sang too. He was gifted in calligraphy. He
was known to be very generous and anyone who fell into bad times
could come to him for financial help. He was larger-than-life and
helped his disciples improve their poetry. He even had a bear as a pet!

Muztar was very close to the Scindia family so when he passed
away in 1927, the Maharajah had him buried in the compound of
Peer Chhingay Shah's dargah [shrine] in Gwalior and not in an
ordinary graveyard.

My father, Jan Nisar Akhtar, had preserved 150 of his father's
ghazals, and then it took me around ten years to gather his poetry
from various sources and finally I got his work published in 2015 in
a five-volume compendium entitled *Khirman.*

NMK: You have both law and poetry in your lineage through your
forefathers. Wouldn't it have been wonderful if we had some first-
person accounts of their lives?

JA: If those accounts are just the telling of an incident, that's not
good enough because incidents are not experiences. For example, if
someone goes for a job interview and says: 'I've been doing the same
work for twenty years, I have twenty years' experience.' You should say
that's wrong—you have one year's experience multiplied by twenty.
Experience is the knowledge and insight you gather from incidents.

All human beings have one seamless story in which one experience
leads to another. When I look at my own life, I see it's a very tight

screenplay. I cannot pick and choose scenes. If I remove scene thirty-two, which happened to be unpleasant, then scene sixty-four, the highlight of the story, would have to be done away with because the two events are connected over time. It's all interwoven, though what is common to all these experiences is you.

NMK: And when is this 'you' formed?

JA: That's like asking a tree when it became a tree. Can you say which part of the tree is the tree? The stump, the trunk, these branches, those leaves, that flower, this fruit? All of it is the tree and so are the unseen roots. Like the many parts of a tree, our life stories are tightly entwined together.

If someone were to ask me if I had a traumatic childhood, I would say my mother's early death changed everything. It was the tragedy that my younger brother Salman and I had to cope with. If she had not died when I was only eight, I would not be the person I am today. My life would have been very different. Losing her early in life shaped me and led me into a particular direction. That loss is a key part of me, a part of my life and a part of my success too.

NMK: Can you tell me about your parents, Safia Akhtar and Jan Nisar Akhtar? By the way, what did you call them?

JA: Ammi and Abbi.

They were married in my maternal grandparents' home in Lucknow in December 1943. A little over nine years later, in January 1953, my mother passed away. So, you could say my parents were married for nine years, though they did not live together for six of those nine years because they were teaching in different cities and could only meet during college holidays.

Another reason they were apart was that my father, who was a member of the Communist Party, had to go underground when the party was banned. An arrest warrant had been issued in his name, so he was forced to leave for Bombay. He quit his college job in Bhopal and left my mother and us brothers there. In the years that my parents lived apart, my mother wrote to him almost every day, and it is thanks to those letters that I have managed to piece together much of the past.

My father had this habit of never throwing away old papers—it's a habit that I share with him, so within a few months of my mother's passing in 1953, he re-read all her letters, one by one. They were so beautifully written that he decided to have them published. In 1955, her letters appeared in a first book called *Zer-e-Lab* [Under the Lips]. A few years later, a second book entitled *Harf-e-Aashna* [Words from Someone Familiar] was released. This book includes eight or nine letters written before she was married, and there are also letters dated to the time they were living together in Bhopal after they were married. *Zer-e-Lab,* which should have been published first, includes letters that speak of her life following my father's departure for Bombay. She also writes of quitting her job in Bhopal and returning to her parents' home in Lucknow when she had fallen ill. Her last letter was written a few days before she died.

My mother's letters were not just the correspondence of a wife writing to her husband about mundane events—here was a vibrant member of society, a woman with political acumen and social ideas, a highly educated woman, an intellectual. It is unsurprising that her letters are regarded as literary masterpieces and became very popular among Urdu readers. Past critics and authors like Krishan Chander, Firaq Gorakhpuri, Razia Sajjad Zaheer and many others have written in glowing terms about them. In the 1960s, I have heard the MA students at Bombay University were asked to write a history of literary letters in Urdu, and this history started from Ghalib and went on to Safia Akhtar.

NMK: Have any of her letters been translated into English?

JA: A selection, but not all.

NMK: How did your parents meet?

JA: My father was known for his poetry from his college days. He was a friend of my mother's elder brother, the great poet Majaz. They were key members of the Progressive Writers' Association along with Sajjad Zaheer, Krishan Chander, Faiz Ahmed Faiz and Sardar Jafri. In addition, my parents had many friends in common. In one of my mother's letters, she writes about their first meeting.

After they got married, circumstances forced my parents to live apart because they found work in different cities. Initially, my father taught Urdu literature at Victoria College in Gwalior, where I later learnt one of his students was Mr Atal Bihari Vajpayee, while my mother at Abdullah Girls' College in Aligarh was also teaching Urdu. She lived in the teachers' hostel and whenever it was possible, she travelled the 217 kilometres between Aligarh and Gwalior to see my father. That's how I came to be born in Gwalior on 17 January 1945 at a hospital in Gwalior.

NMK: You once told me a very interesting story about the day you were born.

JA: The day I was born, my father and his friends came directly from the Communist Party office to the hospital to see my mother and me. One of his friends said: 'When a child is born in a Muslim family, words from the azaan are read into the newborn's ears. But we have different beliefs, so what shall we do?'

My father who was holding the Communist Manifesto in his hand replied: 'All right, then I'll read some lines from the Communist Manifesto into his ear.' And he did. When it came to deciding on a name for me, another friend reminded my father of a poem he had written at the time he was marrying my mother. A line from that poem 'lamha-lamha kisi jaadu ka fasana hoga ... [Every moment will have a magical story]' inspired him to call me 'Jaadu'. Some years later, my parents renamed me Javed when I started kindergarten.

Generally, your real name suggests a pet name, in my case it was the other way round.

My maternal family was equally thrilled by my birth. I was the first child to be born in that family after a long gap of twenty-two years, so it was believed that a wonder child had been born. But then every mother thinks her child is a wonder child and that was how my mother made me feel. By the age of eight, they say your basic personality is signed, sealed and delivered. I'm sure that's true because after that, things started going seriously downhill. [*both laugh*]

NMK: When did your father leave Gwalior?

JA: Around 1947 he moved to Bhopal, where he was appointed the Head of the Department of Urdu at the Government Hamidia Arts and Commerce College. My mother also worked there as a lecturer.

During the holidays we visited my grandparents in Lucknow. Throughout my childhood there were many comings and goings between cities and homes. My mother went back to her parents in Lucknow for the delivery of her second child who was born on 31 July 1946, exactly a year and a half after me. The baby was named Owais. My father then happened to meet a man called Owais some time later and discovered he was a stingy and tightfisted fellow, so he decided his son's name had to be changed. That's how my brother was renamed Salman when he was about three or four years old.

NMK: I understand you lived in Bhopal from the ages of about two to six. What memories do you have of the city?

JA: I have many memories of that time. We lived on the first floor of a house called Mehboob Manzil. It had a wide balcony and Salman and I would stand there every evening to watch our parents returning home. We could see them walking from a long distance away, as the balcony overlooked a huge field called Lal Parade Ground and Hamidia College where they taught was across that field. There were two benches on that balcony—one was blue and the other was a kind of yellow. I loved the colour blue, so I gave the yellow bench to Salman.

I remember Pandit Jawaharlal Nehru had come to Bhopal in 1951 to give a speech at the Lal Parade Ground. It was his first visit to the city after Independence, so they had built a huge stage for him—it's still there. I was not too well that day and could not go with my mother to hear him speak. She found me a pair of binoculars so I could watch Pandit-ji talking on the stage from the balcony. I was about six.

The first general elections in India were held between October 1951 and February 1952. I remember because my mother and many of her colleagues worked as volunteers in the Election Commission—it's still very common for teachers to work as volunteers during elections. Some students joined in too. They worked in our house for hours, opening military-green boxes that arrived in their dozens. On the sides of these boxes, they stuck sheets of paper with symbols of the various political parties printed on them. At the top of the box was a narrow slit through which you could slip in your vote. Do bailon ki jodi [Two bullocks with a yoke] was the symbol of the Congress Party in those days.

I was once asked in kindergarten to draw a flag. The Communist Party had been banned, so what did I do? I drew a red flag and gave it to my teacher, who immediately complained to my mother:

Look what your son has drawn! Be careful, you might lose your job. Don't forget, you're teaching at a government college.

Details of this incident are a bit hazy now, but thankfully my mother talked about it in one of her letters published in *Zer-e-Lab* so I know it did happen. I am sure I drew the red flag because I came from a diehard Communist family. On top of that, I was convinced Stalin was my grandfather, probably because there was a huge portrait of Stalin in our home. I was five at the time and when it finally dawned on me that that was far from the truth, I was totally heartbroken! [*both laugh*]

NMK: What could you tell of your mother's personality through her letters?

JA: Although I lost her when I was only eight, thankfully I have a good memory and can recall so many moments spent with her. Being her son, I am biased, but all those who knew her believed unanimously that she was a person of intellect, knowledge, socio-political awareness, and someone who had a great understanding of literature, particularly when it came to poetry. When I read her letters to my father, I can see the skilful way she uses famous Urdu couplets in her prose—what you cannot miss as well is her wit and sense of humour.

My mother had a great sense of curiosity about different things in the world. In those days plastic had just entered the Indian market, though she had not personally seen it. So she wrote to my father in Bombay, asking him: 'What is plastic? I keep hearing this word. What is it used for? Can you send me some?'

My father duly obliged and sent us a plastic sheet. My mother and a friend of hers examined the sheet carefully. They didn't know what to do with it. Later that week, I saw her cut a small piece from it and try to burn it. It would not burn so she decided to turn the plastic sheet into a bag. She folded it in two and made two holes and threaded two thick woollen strings that served as handles.

My mother's use of the bag was most unusual. She cut out many words from magazines and stuck them onto bits of cardboard and put them into the bag. When I'd come home from school, she would play this game with me, and tell me to take out a cardboard piece and then ask if I could read the word written on it. It was beautiful.

NMK: Your mother showed you much love in the little time she had with you.

JA: [*long pause, overcome with emotion*] Oh, yes.

NMK: Do you remember any of the words you pulled out of that plastic bag?

JA: This may sound very syrupy, but I remember the word 'Dil' [heart]. In Urdu it has a very elegant shape.

When I come to think of it, we lived under one roof as a family for a very short period in my life—only about three years. These three years were the years we spent in Bhopal, before my father had to leave for Bombay. I was about five or six.

NMK: Your mother had a full-time job teaching; did she have any help looking after you and your brother?

JA: Yes, we had a full-time servant; his name was Usmaan. I don't know if you know this but there was a tradition in many families that besides the domestic servants, a family will keep some poor relative in the house; someone who had nowhere to go, no economic support or anything. This person was regarded somewhere between a domestic help and a relative.

I was six and Salman was four-and-a-half and it had become increasingly difficult for my mother to look after us both and teach at the same time. So there was this lady who lived with us—I think she was a distant cousin of my Naani's because we used to call her 'Asroge-wali Naani'. Asroga was a village in UP, from where she came. Children can't really guess the age of adults, though I think she might have been in her late thirties or early forties.

One day, Asroge-wali Naani was going through a box in her room when she took out a small 6x4 inch photo frame. It had a picture of a young boy with images of the zodiac signs stuck all around the photograph. I asked her who the child was, and she said it was her two-year-old son who had died. This stayed in my mind. A two-year-old child dying? And those zodiac signs?

I was thirty years old when *Deewar* was released. The Uttar Pradesh Film Journalists Association gave me an award, which took me to Lucknow after a very long time. During the day I had many interviews and attended a function in the evening. Instead of staying at the hotel that was arranged for me, I went to stay the night at a relative's house. The family was still awake when I got there. I was meeting them after many years, so we sat talking about the past for long hours.

While we were reminiscing, I mentioned Asroge-wali Naani and the fact that she had lived with us when we were kids, and how she had one day showed me the picture of her two-year-old son who had died. An older relative looked perplexed and asked me who I meant. I replied: 'Asroge-wali Naani's son. He died aged two.'

> Are you mad? You're confusing her with someone else. Her husband divorced her because she could not have children.

I was taken aback. What was that photograph all about? And why had she lied to me, a six-year-old child? It was so sad. I suppose we keep nourishing our ambitions and dreams, even if they have failed us. We can't let go of them. Maybe she started believing that was her son. Who knows? She probably cut the picture of the boy and the zodiac signs out of some magazine and framed them. One day, she just disappeared from our lives.

NMK: To go back to your mother and her letter-writing—did she write a lot about you?

JA: Let's say I was an important character in her correspondence. She described many incidents. Apparently, when I was two, I would pick up a newspaper, take the specs off of my uncle Ansar Harwani's face, and put them on. I'd then sit on a chair with a newspaper and pretend that I was reading.

I remember saying as a very young kid that a particular poem reminded me of another poem. My mother overheard me and described the incident in a letter in *Zer-e-Lab*. She wrote how taken aback she was—how could this little kid make such a connection?

NMK: Sounds like you were precocious child! [*both smile*]

JA: Her letters made me very popular among Urdu readers. The women who became fans of my mother's letters wanted to meet her son Jaadu. I became a kind of child star!

NMK: How old were you when you started reading Urdu?

JA: I was very young. Because my grandfather was traditional and religious, he organised a Bismillah ceremony in his house in Lucknow—this ceremony basically marks the start of a child's education.

A Maulvi Sahib came to the house, and a takhti [a wooden tablet] was placed on the table. The Urdu alphabet was written in pencil on it and we children were supposed to dip a reed pen in ink and fill in the alphabet, starting with the letter 'alif'. I got excited and boasted loudly:

Chhapa, chhapa ho jaayega.
[My writing will look like fine print.]

In this state of heightened enthusiasm, I picked up the wrong pen. It had a broad nib, and as I started filling in the first letter of the alphabet, instead of a finely crafted 'alif', a big black blob landed on the takhti.

I burst into tears. You cannot imagine how much I wailed. My family tried to console me by giving me the right pen and persuading me to continue writing. It was a tragic beginning to my education. I still have very bad handwriting and I'm sure it's all because of that unsightly 'alif'! [*both laugh*]

NMK: I am wondering if you were given any pocket money. How much did you get?

JA: My grandfather gave me half an anna in the morning and one anna in the evening. With that I bought Morton's toffees and an aloo tikki for one anna from a fellow who sold chaat near our house. When I moved to my aunt Hamida's home in Aligarh, she gave me five rupees.

NMK: A week?

JA: A month! I'm relieved to tell you it wasn't annually. [*both laugh*] With that money, I paid for an occasional movie and biscuits that I bought during the interval.

NMK: Besides writing, how else did your mother spend her time?

JA: She was a voracious reader and read many novels. While she was reading a novel, she would narrate the story to me when I returned home from school. She would do this chapter by chapter. I suspect that she edited out the romantic scenes. I still remember a story she told me about a Russian boy and a girl who managed to break the supply line of the Nazis in Leningrad. It fascinated me.

My mother was a great music lover and the proud owner of a gramophone. It was very precious to her and was probably the most expensive thing in our house in Bhopal. She owned quite a few 78 rpm records made by a company called 'The Twins'. The records had a yellow label with a picture of two young boys sitting back-to-back.

The landlord of our Bhopal house was known as Thekedar Sahib. He had two wives who lived in the same house. He was in the construction business, hence his name. His family lived on the ground floor, while we rented the first floor. He had a huge display of stylish shoes on a rack in his sitting room. His shoes fascinated me, particularly a pair that had pointed toe caps, a white shoe body and black heel caps—the famous brogues.

NMK: Why were his shoes in the sitting room?

JA: If they were kept in any other room, who would see them? [*both laugh*]

NMK: Were they status symbols?

JA: I think so. I've seen many refrigerators standing proudly in sitting rooms. It used to be quite a common sight because they were considered status symbols. Not everyone could afford a refrigerator, nor could they afford a gramophone.

NMK: Was your mother's gramophone the wind-up type?

JA: Yes. Although she owned a gramophone, we didn't have a radio. But our landlord did, and sometimes we could hear music drifting up to our balcony. One day, my mother heard the strains of a song. She rushed to the balcony and stood there listening with rapt attention. I remember watching her as she looked far into the distance. I was intrigued by how absorbed she was in the words of a song from *Mahal*.

NMK: *Mahal* was a 1949 film. That means you were about four or five years old. By any chance was it the famous Lata Mangeshkar song 'Aayega aanewala [The one who was meant to return will come back some day]'?

JA: No, it was Rajkumari's 'Ghabra ke jo hum sar ko takraayen toh achcha ho. Iss jeene mein sau dukh hain mar jaayen toh achcha ho. [There are a thousand sorrows in this life, dying is better than living]'.

In February 1982, there was a huge musical programme called 'Mortal Men Immortal Melodies' organised by Siddharth Kak at the Shanmukhananda Hall in Bombay. I wrote the commentary on the history of Indian film music for the show and Shabana was compering. I did not think many people had even heard of Rajkumari, who was an old lady by then, but when she sang the first line: 'Ghabra ke jo hum sar ko ...' She had not got to the second line when the hall erupted with applause. Everyone clapped and clapped. There must have been some magic in that song.

NMK: I happened to attend that show too. The wonderful Mr P.K. Nair, who was the Founding Director of the National Film Archive of India in Pune, invited me to go with him. It was such a historical event for the film world because Noor Jehan had come to India after a 35-year gap. She sang 'Awaaz de kahaan hai' to thunderous applause. Later, Dilip Kumar and she reminisced about the past on stage.

Besides film songs, what other kinds of music did your mother like?

JA: Indian classical music and ghazals. To be honest, when we were children, we could not tell the difference between a film song and a ghazal, because many film songs sounded like ghazals back then.

NMK: When your father was forced to leave for Bombay to avoid getting arrested, how did your mother make ends meet?

JA: She applied for my father's job when he left for Bombay. The interview went well, and she was appointed the new Head of the Department of Urdu at Hamidia College in Bhopal. By the way, the college principal, Mr P.C. Malhotra, was the father of the famous playback singer Sudha Malhotra.

It became increasingly difficult for my mother to manage working while looking after me and my brother, so I was sent to Lucknow to my grandfather's house where my Aunt Hamida took care of me. In fact, I was brought up by two ladies, my mother who I called 'Ammi' and Aunt Hamida who I called 'Amma'. I continued to call her 'Amma', even when she was ninety-three years old.

Amma was a second mother to me, so much so that my Naani got very worried and used to say:

> What is happening? This boy is calling my unmarried daughter 'Amma'. Who is going to marry her? People will think he is her son.

Amma did get married, and she married Abu Salim when I was four. I wasn't too well at that time and was suffering from kaali khaansi [whooping cough], but all the same I remember flashes of their wedding preparations.

I must tell you some more about Amma. She did an MA in Economics at Aligarh Muslim University in 1947 and a second masters at the University of London. She was a Professor of Economics. In 1955, she wrote a fine and insightful article in memory of Majaz called *Jaggan Bhaiya*, which was translated into English by Sami Rafiq entitled *Majaz, My Brother*. He was only forty-four when he passed away and she was eleven years younger than him. Majaz was affectionately called 'Jaggan' by all the family members because he was an insomniac.

Amma was a formidable woman. When she was eighty years old she decided to become a writer. Her first book was *Shorish-e-Dauran* [The Turmoil of Times]. It was a kind of sociological study of life in the small kasbah of Rudauli, where our zamindar forefathers lived and where she was born and raised. She described the culture, rituals and daily lives of people in the early twentieth century and wrote about how Muslim zamindars celebrated Diwali and other Hindu festivals.

NMK: Do you remember if you minded being sent away from your mother to Lucknow?

JA: I don't believe I minded. My grandparents' house was full of aunties and uncles, and they pampered me to no end. The house was bigger too. In 1951, my mother had to leave her job and moved back from Bhopal to her parents' home in Lucknow when she fell very ill. I was about six-and-a-half then.

During the time we were living with my grandparents, I became very close to my maternal grandmother.

NMK: You have often talked about her. She sounds like an amazing woman.

JA: Naani was amazing. She only spoke Awadhi and could not speak Urdu, Hindi or Hindustani. Her sons and daughters were highly educated and intelligent and though they were also fluent in Urdu and English, they also knew Awadhi. Her husband's name was Siraj-ul Haq. They had five children: Aarfa, Majaz, Ansar Harwani, Safia and Hamida.

NMK: Did you ever visit your grandparents' house in Rudauli as a child?

JA: My grandfather took me to a very important dargah in Rudauli. I have vague memories of a fair and an Urs. It was during that trip that we visited the family house. I remember it clearly. I was travelling in a doli [palanquin] with some female members of the family.

I went back there briefly in my late fifties. The house had been converted into a girls' school, though I could still recall the layout from the old days—the sprawling veranda, the winding staircase, the old terrace.

NMK: Can you tell me something about Aarfa, your eldest aunt?

JA: She was very young when her husband died, so she moved back to Lucknow to her parents' home. She had one son called Abdul Maroof Nomani. Everybody used to call him Abbu Bhai. He and his wife called Dulhan Bhabhi were very kind to Salman and me. He contracted polio in his childhood and walked with a limp. He was a wonderful person. In later life he worked at the Income Tax Department and was a fanatically honest man. He held a high position in Kanpur, which was perhaps the most industrialised city in UP then. He refused to take a single rupee in bribes, and this made his children rather unhappy with him because the children of his juniors owned Lambrettas while Abdul Maroof Nomani could not afford even a bicycle. My cousin was twenty-one years older than me.

NMK: Ah! So, he was the son after whom, twenty-one years later, you were born in your maternal family.

JA: Yes, that's right.

NMK: I see now. You were saying you were close to your grandmother...

JA: I spent a lot of time with Naani and that's why I can speak Awadhi. When I was a toddler, I used to sleep next to her. Naani knew only one bedtime story and every night she repeated the same story, and every night I showed the same enthusiasm, as though it was the first time that I was hearing it. Her convoluted story was about two sisters, Khera and Bera. It was the weirdest story I have ever heard. It was long-winded and had no structure; it's too long to recount here. But Naani loved it, and I was happy that she loved telling it to me. If I ever make an autobiographical film like Federico Fellini's *Amarcord*, I'd definitely have the Khera and Bera story in it.

I learnt much later that my grandmother, whose name was Nabi Bakshi, was the only daughter of a zamindar. In her childhood, a maulvi was called to the house to make her study, but she refused. So, her father decided to abandon the idea of educating her—in any case, he didn't think she was going to apply for a job, so why would she need an education in the first place? That was the reasoning.

As a result, my grandmother was illiterate. Nevertheless, this completely illiterate woman had a thirst for knowledge. A servant was assigned to her whose main task was reading the newspaper, *Qaumi Awaz,* out loud. She would sit on her bed, cutting supari while listening intently to every word, from first to last page—and she did this every single day. She had strong political views and shared them freely with her sons, often disagreeing with them. By the way, Pandit Nehru founded *Qaumi Awaz* in 1937. The paper folded in 2008, but its digital version lives on. Its sister publications are the *National Herald* in English and *Navjivan* in Hindi.

NMK: Did your grandparents give you a religious education?

JA: Because I could read well, my grandfather gave me a biography of the Prophet that was written for children. It opened a whole new universe for me—the Arab tribes, the chieftains, their battles, the angel who talked to the Prophet—it was a world of great mystery and adventure for a six-year-old. I found it fascinating.

The only family members I saw praying were my grandparents. About a year after my mother died, I must have been about nine, my grandfather gave me an ayat [verse] from the Quran and said: 'If you learn this by heart, I'll give you eight annas.' I memorised it and he gave me eight annas. A few days later, he gave me another ayat with the promise of a rupee.

I remember an incident that will show you how very unusual and exceptional my Naani was. One day, she happened to overhear my grandfather asking me to learn yet another ayat. Here was a deeply religious lady who had an innate capacity of rising above her own faith and seeing the bigger picture. She was furious and told her husband:

> You have no right to give him a religious education. Can you imagine if his mother were alive today, would she have taught him an ayat? If Jaadu was living with his father in Bombay, do you think his father would teach him this? This orphaned child is living with us. We have no right to impose our religion on our grandson.

So that was the end of my religious education!

How magnanimous my Naani was. Just think of her in light of today where there is so much intolerance and cynicism. She was an uneducated woman who could not even sign her own name and was so religious herself—praying five times a day, come rain or shine—and yet this lady showed such large-heartedness and objectivity when she told her husband: 'We have no right to impose our religion on our grandson.'

I did not fully appreciate Naani's greatness of spirit until I was older. My deep respect and admiration for her grew over time, and I wish a fraction of this generosity of spirit existed in the political leaders in the world today.

NMK: So, that was the end of your religious education? I hope it wasn't the end of your reading!

JA: No, no! I was an avid read. I remember reading the children's books published by Maktaba Jamia. Among them was a story written by the former President Dr Zakir Husain called 'Abbu Khan ki Bakri'. It was an interesting tale about a goat called Chandni. Another short story I also recall is 'Mazdoor ka Beta' by Syed Mohammad Mohsin. It was about the son of a poor labourer determined to study, who would sit under a streetlamp and read his textbooks.

NMK: Were your grandparents well-off?

JA: Yes. They were zamindars from Rudauli, which is in the Barabanki district, about 90 kilometres from Lucknow. My grandfather was the first person in the area to be educated. He had two degrees: a BA and an LLB. His family was not keen for him to get a job. For zamindars, getting a job was seen as below their status, but Naana insisted he wanted to work, and his parents finally agreed.

My grandfather got a government job and rose in the ranks to become an Excise Commissioner. By a strange coincidence, Shabana's grandfather was also an Excise Commissioner in another part of India. [*smiles*]

When it came to his own children, my grandfather made sure they were educated, and that included the girls of the family. In his book, *From Pluralism to Separatism: Qasbas in Colonial Awadh* (2004), the historian Mushirul Hasan wrote about some relatives from Rudauli who once visited Lucknow and tried to find my grandfather's house. They asked a passer-by if he knew the house belonging to the gentleman whose daughter had a BA degree. The passer-by instantly led our relatives to the right house. Having an educated daughter was a big deal then. It set you socially apart.

NMK: Where was your grandparents' home in Lucknow?

JA: In Civil Lines, New Hyderabad. My grandfather's name was Siraj-ul Haq, so the name of the house was Dar-ul Siraj [House of Siraj].

It was a name given by Majaz. About twelve years ago, someone told me the gate nameplate had been removed and was stored in some warehouse. The next time I visited Lucknow I managed to retrieve it, and it now hangs on a wall alongside photographs of the family in my Khandala house.

NMK: What about your ancestral land in Rudauli? Who looked after it?

JA: My Naana had a manager; I believe his name was Chedi Lal. I'm sure Salman will remember. Chedi Lal used to come to Lucknow with huge sacks of mangoes and grain. It was my grandmother who did the accounts and who looked after the affairs of the farm.

NMK: You were eight when you lost your mother. That must have been hugely traumatic.

JA: My mother, Salman and I were together at my grandparents' in Lucknow for about a year and a half before her condition worsened. She was suffering from an autoimmune disease called scleroderma. It's a rare and painful disease. At the end of her life, she was unable to even hold a pen in her hands. I remember her hands. She died on 18 January 1953. She was only thirty-seven. It was a day after my eighth birthday. Salman was six-and-a-half. That's no age to lose your mother.

There's a very sad story, though I must tell it to you. The graveyard where my mother was buried was about a mile away from my grandparents' house—after my mother was buried, it was decided they would have the grave cemented over. My cousin Abdul Maroof Nomani, who we called Abbu Bhai, was responsible for getting the job done. I don't know who told me, but someone said that while the men were cementing the grave, I could see my mother. I took Salman by the hand—remember I was eight and he was six-and-a-half—and we slipped out of the house and walked the mile to the graveyard.

Abbu Bhai was talking to the workers when suddenly he saw us. For young children a mile is a long distance and after my cousin got over the shock of seeing us there on our own, he asked us to sit down and made us drink some water. A few minutes later, he said we must be hungry, and it was better that we went home and returned after lunch. He said we would see our mother then.

Salman and I walked home and had our lunch. After lunch, we sneaked out again and headed to the graveyard. By the time we got there, all the work was all done, and my mother's grave had been cemented over. My cousin consoled us by saying:

They had to finish the work. You're late. I want to tell you I saw your mother and she's fine.

He was lying of course. [*long pause*] Almost seventy years have passed since my mother passed away, and it's not as though I cry every day when I think of her, but when I do, it still hurts. It's so strange. I am a grandfather now—my granddaughters are much older than I was when I lost my mother. It is illogical, irrational that a seventy-seven-year-old man still gets tears in his eyes when he remembers his thirty-six-year-old mother. A mother who was younger than my own children are now. My rational being tells me it's stupid, yet it still hurts me deeply. Perhaps I did not allow myself to grieve when I should have.

NMK: Why didn't you grieve as a child?

JA: I could not afford to. I don't believe I could have hung onto my energy and zeal through the years. Maybe I would've been consumed by self-pity. Sometimes, you develop a defence mechanism that saves you and tells you, 'No, don't go that way.'

NMK: I'm guessing you covered your hurt in part through humour.

JA: Maybe.

NMK: When your mother passed away, I imagine your grandparents and your mother's younger sister, Aunt Hamida, became entirely responsible for your upbringing.

JA: Yes, to a great extent.

NMK: Was it during these years in Lucknow that you got to know your uncle, the poet Majaz?

JA: Yes. We used to call him 'Bade Mamu Sahib', and we called our other uncle, Ansar Harwani, 'Chhote Mamu Sahib'.

They say Majaz was a moody child and something of a loner. As a young man, he was a very popular poet. In fact, he was a star poet and was among the first Urdu poets of the Progressive Writers' Movement. He was born in October 1911 in Rudauli and was a man way ahead of his time—just imagine, in the late 1930s, early 1940s, he was writing poetry about women's empowerment, capitalism, and he had even written an anthem for freedom against British Rule.

Majaz and Faiz were contemporaries and good friends, though Majaz started writing political poetry before Faiz. Both poets were bestowed with great talent, but I suppose discipline, focus and age favoured Faiz and so he attained incredible heights.

In his youth, Bade Mamu Sahib was a good-looking man and I remember Ismat Chughtai once writing about how college girls kept his books under their pillows and had bets on which girl might be the first to have an affair with him. [*laughs*] He fell in love with an upper-class married woman in Delhi, but their relationship had no future and despite various attempts by the family to get him married, he never did.

People know Majaz as a great romantic poet, but there is another side to him that is not widely known and that was his great love for sports. In his schooldays he played hockey, and at college he played tennis. He was very knowledgeable about sports. He was the one who got me interested in the subject. There was no television at that time, so we listened to Test Matches on the radio. I must have been about seven or eight, almost too young to even understand the commentary, despite that we were glued to the radio.

Bade Mamu Sahib was very close to my mother and after she died, he spent even more time with us. I think he felt responsible for Salman and me. We were very fond of him too. At nights we ran excitedly into his room and laid down on his bed on either side of him. He told us about all the great sportsmen, including the magnificent hockey player Dhyan Chand. He described his matches to us, goal by goal. It was almost as if we were watching Dhyan Chand in action. He became a huge star in our eyes. Bade Mamu Sahib also spoke about the formidable Don Bradman. Mushtaq Ali, the Indian cricketer, was another sportsman my uncle greatly admired. We fell in love with cricket, thanks to him.

One day, out of the blue, he asked me to go with him across the road to the house opposite ours. He introduced me to Mohan, who was the young son of a respected and traditional Kayastha family. Even though the boy was the same age as me, everybody called him Mohan-ji. My uncle introduced me to Mohan-ji's father, Ballu Babu, and to Chowdhary Sahib, Mohan-ji's grandfather. Three generations of the family lived together in that house—grandfather, father and son. Mohan-ji's cousin, Jai, and I became close friends. He died a few years ago and his son Sharat Choudhary and I are still in touch. He lives in Lucknow and is doing well. He still treats me with the same respect that he would show to a real uncle.

Once Bade Mamu Sahib had introduced us to our neighbours, he said we kids should get together and start a cricket club. Promptly Mohan-ji, Jai, some other boys from the neighbourhood and I formed a club. Fortunately, next to our house, there was a large empty patch of unclaimed land. We cleared it up and this became our cricket field. This great poet called Majaz not only gave us the idea to start a cricket club but he also named it the Jai Hind Club!

The illustrious members of the Jai Hind Club were all of eight or nine years old, and could often be found playing cricket. Jai and Mohan-ji, who were richer than we were, provided the bat and ball. As Jai owned the ball, we could not judge him LBW, because if we did, he'd take his ball and go home. So, it was only natural that Jai enjoyed this immunity.

My uncle also taught us how to play pachisi. It's a kind of Ludo. Instead of a board and dice, you have kauris [shells] that you throw onto a fabric shaped like a cross. The team that reaches the finish line first wins. We loved playing pachisi. Majaz could draw well too and drew pictures for us.

NMK: I read somewhere that he had psychological problems.

JA: Yes. He had a few nervous breakdowns. I remember the day he returned home from a mental asylum in Ranchi. I was too young to recall all the details, though I do remember a writer friend of his, Suhail Azimabadi, had brought him home. My grandmother who adored Majaz—in fact he was her favourite son—hugged him for a long time with tears in her eyes.

NMK: Was he better when he returned from Ranchi?

JA: He was. Though he soon started drinking again. It's tragic. Majaz and Faiz were two important poets of their time. But Faiz had a huge sense of discipline. You need discipline with talent. The third important thing is self-esteem. Sometimes, a person who by temperament is a big man, though with modest talent, is pushed forward by his sense of discipline, so he will create a place for himself in his given field. At other times, you can have someone with enormous talent who is an undisciplined and petty person. But the power of their talent usually allows their flaws to be forgotten. I am thinking of the poet Firaq Gorakhpuri. He had such immense talent that ultimately his personality and indiscipline could not stop him from achieving recognition as a great poet.

Rarely does it happen that talent, discipline and self-esteem come together. Besides Ghalib, Faiz Ahmed Faiz is another example of someone who had all three qualities.

NMK: Did you ever meet Faiz Sahib?

JA: I cannot say I spent any time with him, although the time I did spend with him is unbelievable. So improbable that I am relieved to say the incident was confirmed by Faiz Sahib's daughter Salima Hashmi. She was a professor at the National College of Arts in Lahore and is a celebrated painter in Pakistan. If I had recounted this story to anyone without having her having confirmed it with her father, no one would have believed me.

It was in 1967–1968. Faiz Sahib was coming to Bombay after a gap of almost twenty years, and there was a lot of excitement about his arrival. Faiz is coming! Faiz is coming!

In those days, I was living in Kamal Studio, and heard about the grand mushaira to be held at Rang Bhavan, near St. Xavier's College. It's an open-air auditorium. I was totally dejected because I didn't have the money to even travel to Rang Bhavan, leave alone buying a ticket for the mushaira. And Faiz was coming!

I was downcast and frustrated and sat drinking with a few friends in some drinking joint. I got quite drunk and decided to hell with it, I'm going to the mushaira. I went to Andheri station, took a local train without a ticket, got down at Marine Lines, and walked from the station to Rang Bhavan. There was no one at the gate as it was much after the start time. I slipped through the back door leading to the stage and managed to walk onto the back of the stage. I sat down on the row of bolsters placed behind the poets who were at the mic reciting their verse. When you're drunk, you can't hear too well, and you feel very sleepy. The poets' voices started to fade into the distance, and drunk as I was, I fell into a deep sleep, leaning against the bolsters. When I suddenly woke up, I realised the mushaira had just finished, and everyone was leaving the auditorium. I looked up and saw Faiz being taken towards a car. A huge crowd had surrounded him. I ran quickly towards them and shouted at the organisers:

What the hell are you doing? Why can't you control the crowd?
Faiz Sahib, please come this way. Follow me.

I took charge! I directed him to the car waiting for him, made him sit on the back seat, and quickly slid next to him. With great authority, I instructed the driver: 'Let's go!' A young man from the organisers' team was sitting in the front seat and he assumed I was Faiz Sahib's friend, so he told the driver to head to Hotel Gulmarg. And so this great poet and I talked about poetry till we got to the hotel. There, the young man asked whether Faiz Sahib needed the car:

Shall we keep the driver, or let it go, Faiz Sahib?
Let him go. Where will I go out now? Miyan, get the room keys for me.

He called me 'Miyan' throughout our interaction because he did not know my name, and amazingly had not asked for it. With the room keys in my hand, we went upstairs, sat in his hotel suite, and ordered some whiskey. We were drinking and discussing the intricacies of the Urdu alphabet when Ali Sardar Jafri and Majrooh Sultanpuri arrived and joined us for a round of drinks. They assumed that Faiz Sahib knew me.

I hadn't completely recovered from my earlier drunken state, and as I continued drinking, I started to feel very sleepy. I told Faiz Sahib I could not keep my eyes open, and he said: 'Go inside and sleep.' I went to the other room which had twin beds and collapsed on one of them. I had no idea when the others left.

When I opened my eyes the next morning, I was stone-cold sober. I continued lying on the bed with my head covered by a sheet. I could hear a press conference in full progress in that very same room. The main organiser of the mushaira, Kulsum Sayani, Ameen Sayani's mother, was talking to Faiz Sahib and saying:

We learnt you were not getting the NOC to visit India, so I called General Ayub, and I asked him what he was doing ... Faiz Sahib, who is sleeping on the other bed?

Faiz Sahib stuttered and stammered: 'Actually, he is ...' He quickly changed the subject:

When you called General Ayub a day earlier, they had already sent me the NOC ...
Thank God because here your fans and admirers were dying to see you in person ... who is this gentleman?

Faiz Sahib changed the subject again:

He is ... it's the love of my fans and admirers that has brought me here. I am so grateful to them.

Their conversation continued in much the same way, and still hiding under the bed sheet, I decided to take the plunge. I suddenly got up and said:

Faiz Sahib, main chalta hoon. [Faiz Sahib, I'm leaving]
Haan Miyan, aap jaaiye. [Yes, Miyan. You can go]

And before anyone could say Faiz Ahmed Faiz, I was out of the room!

NMK: Wow! That was a close shave. Quite an amazing story!

JA: In 1977–1978, I went to Karachi, and that's where I met Salima Hashmi for the first time. I told her about this incredible encounter—how I got into the car next to her father, had a drink in his hotel suite, the others arrived, I fell asleep and rushed out of there in the morning. She laughed and said:

It's typical of my father not to have the guts to ask you who you were!

When Salima-ji asked her father about this incident, he said he knew who I was, but he didn't really. He was too embarrassed to admit it to her.

NMK: Did you meet Faiz Sahib again?

JA: Yes, he came to Bombay in 1978. Sabir Dutt, the editor and publisher of the magazine *Fann aur Shakhsiyat* was releasing a special volume on Faiz's personality and poetry, and Sabir Dutt asked me if he could release his publication in my house—by then I was living in a bungalow on Bandstand. Faiz Sahib and all the important poets attended the function.

Later he sent me his last collection of poetry inscribing it with these words: 'Jaadu Miyan ke liye, pyaar se [With love to Jaadu Miyan]'. I still have the book. It's very precious to me.

I always found it remarkable how well Faiz Sahib could handle criticism, and how generously he credited his contemporaries. Only a large-hearted person can do that. He was never known to boast either. He was the brightest star of the Progressive Writers' Movement. He spent many years in jail in Pakistan and wrote much of his poetry behind bars, but his hypnotic verse made even a prison sound like a romantic place.

If you read Ghalib's letters, you'll know he was a man with a big vision, great talent, focus and impressive personality, and you can say the same about Faiz. These are the traits of big people. Some might say Ghalib was a drunkard, or he had an affair with someone or the other, or that he gambled. None of this really matters. His vision was big. When Sir Syed Ahmad Khan, who founded the Aligarh Muslim University (AMU), was translating Akbar's constitution, which spoke of the greatness of Mughal times, Ghalib said we should all look to the future and not the past. He wrote this sher which reflects his thinking:

> Imaan mujhe roke hai jo kheenche hai mujhe kufr
> Kaaba mere peechhe hai kaleesa mere aage
> [Faith stops me while heresy pulls me along. Behind me stands the
> Kaaba, ahead of me the church.]

In this context the Kaleesa is the symbol of Western tradition, not of the church. And Kaaba is the symbol of traditionalism and not the place in Saudi Arabia.

NMK: If you were interviewing the great poet Ghalib, what would you ask him?

JA: People around the world who are familiar with Urdu literature and poetry believe that Ghalib was the greatest poet of the nineteenth century in the world. If I had met him I would have asked him:

Sir, ijaazat ho toh hum bhi kuchh shayari kar lein? [Sir, if you permit us, can we write a little poetry too?] [*both laugh*]

NMK: Coming back to your own family's huge contribution to Urdu poetry, did your uncle Majaz write till the end of his life?

JA: No, he stopped about ten years before he died in 1955. All his poetry was written in his twenties and thirties.

I am quite certain that my family genes are not compatible with alcohol. The family members who were drawn to alcohol have done great harm to themselves. They drank too much and became alcoholics. My other uncle, Ansar Harwani, drank too much as well. At a later stage in his life, he became a teetotaller, though it was too late.

NMK: Ansar Harwani does sound like a fascinating personality. To be so involved at such a young age in politics is unusual.

JA: That's right. He was a strong-minded young man. At fourteen he announced to the family that he wanted to be part of the freedom movement and ran away from home to join Gandhi-ji. When Gandhi-ji saw this teenager, he told him: 'Go back home, finish your studies, then come back.' And that's what my uncle did.

K.A. Abbas has written a lot about him in his autobiography *I Am Not An Island*. They were classmates at AMU and very good friends. Back then, debating contests between universities were major events and my uncle and K.A. Abbas were in the team representing AMU. Russi Karanjia was the debater from Bombay University.

In later years, my uncle and Abbas Sahib worked together as journalists at *The Bombay Chronicle,* which was founded by Pherozeshah Mehta and edited by B.G. Horniman. Abbas Sahib's popular column, 'Last Page' first appeared in *The Bombay Chronicle* in 1935 and then moved to *Blitz* when *The Bombay Chronicle* shut down. It was the same Russi Karanjia who, in 1941, along with B.G. Horniman and Dinkar Nadkarni founded *Blitz,* a weekly investigative magazine.

NMK: Can you tell me a bit more about your uncle, Ansar Harwani?

JA: At one point, he was rusticated from university because of his role in the freedom movement. Getting rusticated did not dampen his spirits and he continued editing pamphlets and newsletters while actively participating in the Quit India Movement. He was only twenty-three when he was inducted into the Congress Central Committee that had prominent members like Jawaharlal Nehru, Sardar Patel, J.B. Kripalani, Jayaprakash Narayan, Maulana Azad and Subhas Chandra Bose.

He was more of a follower of Subhas Chandra Bose than he was of Gandhi-ji. He became very close to Netaji over the years and always took his side in any argument. Ansar Harwani was the founder of the All India Youth League and the General Secretary of the All India Students Federation between 1936 and 1939. When Netaji left the Congress to form the Forward Bloc, he joined him.

Ansar Harwani wrote a couple of books, including *Before Freedom and After,* in which he quoted his mother as saying:

> Although my mother was illiterate, she had perhaps more political expediency than I ever did. She used to tell me—you're wrong. You should not follow Netaji, follow Gandhi-ji. You should listen to him.

In *Before Freedom and After*, he even mentions me. At one time he was incarcerated in an Allahabad prison and was going to be transferred to another jail. The train in which he was travelling was going to pass through Lucknow and so a well-wisher at the Allahabad prison informed my grandparents that the family could meet him for a few minutes if they came to the Lucknow railway station at a given time. My grandmother and my mother, with me in her arms, waited on the platform for the train to pull in. They found the compartment where my uncle was sitting. His guards were kind enough to allow him to hold me. He was wearing handcuffs and described the scene in his book:

> My mother and my sister Safia came to see me. My sister brought along her child whom I had not seen before. He was about six months old. That was the first time I saw my nephew.

Ansar Harwani was arrested again near the Arakan mountains in Burma. On 14 August 1947, he was released from a Calcutta prison. He was a Member of Parliament for ten years and died in 1996 in Delhi aged eighty.

NMK: Do you think your uncle's interest in politics informed your interest in politics?

JA: I was born in that house—in that family, so I had politics on one side and poetry and literature on the other. It was natural that I'd be influenced by both.

NMK: How aware were you of the great Indian writers early in life?

JA: There was a lot of comings and goings to our home when I was a child—many writers and poets came to stay. I must have seen Krishan Chander in my childhood too. When he had come to Bhopal for the Progressive Writers' Conference, he and Ismat Chughtai stayed with us. I later read the article Ismat Apa wrote on that conference, in which she wittily commented: 'Safia has gone out and has lit her two lamps on my grave.' What she meant was that my mother had left her two sons, me and Salman, in her care when stepping out.

Coming back to Krishan Chander, in later years, I read the keynote lecture he gave at the Progressive Writers' Conference in Bhopal. It was brilliant. Though I must admit, it was only when I was about nine that I became consciously aware of Krishan Chander as a writer.

I was studying in the sixth standard at Colvin Taluqdars' College in Lucknow and one day my Urdu teacher asked us to write an essay on 'Subah ka Manzar'. It means the scenery of the morning, or you could say the morning atmosphere. I had no idea what early morning really was, though I remember the servants used to say they could hear the roar of the lion at 4 a.m. every morning, even though the zoo was across the river in Banarasi Bagh, some miles away from our home in Civil Lines.

I never personally heard the lion roaring, although the very idea fascinated me. To even imagine it was exciting. So, I started my essay with these words: 'Early in the morning, the roar of the lion could be heard. I wonder whether the people who live closer to the zoo can hear the growling of a bear ...'

When Amma saw me writing, she grabbed the essay from my hands and read it out loud, then threw the papers on the ground. She was furious and said: 'Do you think you are Krishan Chander? You think you can just sit down and write free hand?' Now what is free hand? I don't know! Though I know she used that term—free hand.

Amma then told everyone in the house: 'This boy thinks he's Krishan Chander. He thinks he can write an essay spontaneously. Who does he think he is? Just look at him!' When I heard her, I thought to myself: 'Who is Krishan Chander? If he can write on "Subah ka Manzar", he must be very talented.' I did not connect him to the visitor who stayed with us when I was younger.

Once Amma made it clear to me what makes a good writer, she sat down and wrote: 'In the early morning when the farmer heads towards his field carrying a plough on his shoulders, we hear the oxen bells ring out ...' It was all fake, unreal, and not my experience. But I had no choice, I could not argue with her and submitted her essay, passing it off as my own. I still believe mine was better!

NMK: I wish she hadn't thrown your essay away! What finally happened to Dar-ul Siraj, the Lucknow house?

JA: The house still stands though it belongs to another family. Dar-ul Siraj had a big compound with all kinds of trees, including a mango, a papaya and two Ashoka and two guava trees. One of the guava trees was tall and the branches were too high for us kids to climb, while the other tree had low-hanging branches that were well within our reach. Guava trees have hard wood and if you sat on a branch, even a slender one, it was unlikely to snap. That is why the guava tree became a special tree to me, and a friend to all the family children who visited my grandparents' house during the school holidays. We formed a little group that included two of Amma's children, Sumbul and Irfan, Shahid, a second cousin who is now in California, Abbu Bhai's two children, Asma and Urfi, and Salman and me.

And how can I forget the daughter of the female family cook? Her name was Hamida, though everyone called her Chhutkaniya. She had an older sister called Saeeda, who was known as Badhkaniya. Chhutkaniya was about twelve and was the real leader of the group. She was a naughty girl! She told us all about the birds and the bees. We kids had no real clue. We were about eight or nine, though I must say we had our suspicions! We thought there must be something that makes the world go round. I don't know what Chhutkaniya knew but she seemed to know it all. Much later I came to know her information was not very scientific!

On the days when a hot wind blew and the doors and windows of the house were closed while the older members of the family took an afternoon nap, we kids, along with Chhutkaniya, slipped out of the house and perched on our favourite branch of that guava tree and spent hours chatting. It was our living room.

When I visited Lucknow a few years ago, the new owners of Dar-ul Siraj invited me over so I could see the old house. They had made a few changes to the house itself, but the guava tree was gone. I felt as though I had lost a close relative. The house will never be the same for me without it or Chhutkaniya. I still miss them.

NMK: Did you see Chhutkaniya again?

JA: After many years, I had to go to Lucknow for the filming of a documentary that was being made on me and I met her. She was a grandmother, yet her gutsy attitude had not changed. She didn't care about me having become someone famous and gave the most candid interview. I have it on video somewhere.

A couple of years later I went to Lucknow and enquired about her. I was told she was unwell, so I went to her house to see her. She was lying on a bed and clutching onto a bottle of medicine as though it was going to save her life. When she saw me, she started crying. I got my friend Jai to transfer her to a hospital and paid all the expenses. She died a few days later and with her went a little part of my childhood.

NMK: In 1956, when you were about ten years old and living in your grandparents' home, you decided to move with your Aunt Hamida and her husband Abu Salim to Aligarh while Salman stayed with your grandparents. Why did you decide to move with your aunt?

JA: As I told you she was like a mother to me. Amma had looked after me for years and was the only one who could control me to some extent. When she decided to leave her teaching job at a girls' college in Lucknow and join her husband in Aligarh, moving with her was a natural choice.

NMK: How was leaving Lucknow?

JA: I remember a strange scene. When we moved from our Bhopal house all my mother's belongings were moved to my grandparents' home in Lucknow. My mother had a lot of crockery and various other household things, and Amma who probably needed some stuff because she was going to set up a new home in Aligarh said my mother's possessions should be divided between us two brothers.

Everything was laid out in the courtyard. On one side Abu Bhai's wife, Dulhan Bhabhi, sat with Salman and on the other side, I was made to sit next to Amma. One piece went to Salman, then one piece to me. Amma guided me as to what I should pick. When I chose the gramophone instead of a dinner set because I had an emotional attachment to it, as it was tied to my mother's love of music, this upset Amma. She later said: 'What's the point of choosing a gramophone?'

Think how insensitive and damaging it is for children to be pitted against each other to choose their mother's possessions in this way. Dulhan Bhabhi was an unwilling participant in this game. Anyway, that is how the gramophone came in my share and when I left with Amma for Aligarh, I insisted it come along with me.

I now owned the wind-up gramophone, though I did not have any records. I somehow managed to buy a single 78 rpm. It was from the film *Kanhaiya*. On one side there was the song 'Mujhe tum se kuchh bhi na chhahiye' by Mukesh [*JA sings*] and on the flip side was Lata Mangeshkar's 'O Kanhaiya'. When I finally left Aligarh some years later, I could not carry that large gramophone box with me, so Salman became the proud owner of it. That's why we both have different memories associated with my mother's gramophone.

NMK: How were the years you spent with your aunt and uncle in Aligarh?

JA: Soon after we arrived there, they admitted me to Minto Circle. The school building resembled a castle and dated back to the British era. We lived in a house on the edge of the city; it had a huge empty stretch of land in front of our bungalow, and on the other side stood our neighbours' house. Away from these two houses there was a kind of jungle and some small villages.

My neighbours were a lovely family—the father was a retired police officer called Mina Zuberi. He had quite a few children and I was great friends with two of them—Hajra, who was three years older than me, and Rabia, who was five years older. Hajra was a painter and Rabia was a very good sculptor. In fact, one of her sculptures won the first prize in the Youth Festival.

In 1961, the Zuberi family migrated to Pakistan and there Rabia founded the Karachi School of Arts. In Pakistan, she is sometimes referred to as the Queen of Arts. They were talented sisters and their younger brother, Mohsin, was my classmate. He joined the Merchant Navy in Pakistan and often came to Bombay, and we met. We were in the same gymnastics team in our school days, and we used to play cricket together. I was the opening batsman.

I visited Karachi in 1979 and met the two Zuberi sisters. I had not seen them for years. Rabia invited me to the Karachi School of Arts and showed me around. Hajra was still painting; she had married a Bengali gentleman who was also a painter.

Rabia remained unmarried. She told me she had faced some problems as some people thought she was teaching people how to make statues, which is haraam [forbidden] in Islam. She explained that every statue was not for idol worship and that statues could also be art. She asked her critics, 'What do you think of dolls that children play with? Are they haraam or halaal?'

They were lovely people. I remember them well. Mohsin, my classmate, has passed away. I have lost touch with the Zuberi sisters now.

NMK: In the days you were living with your Aunt Hamida in Aligarh, you were a great fan of Dev Anand's. Shabana once showed me a picture of you in your teenage years dressed like the star. You looked just like him!

JA: [*smiles*] I was thirteen when I saw *Munimji*. I was crazy about Dev Anand. Before that I was mad about Dilip Kumar after seeing

Aan and *Udan Khatola*. [*JA sings*] 'O door ke musaafir humko bhi saath le le, hum reh gaye akele.' Then I saw *Shree 420* and started loving Raj Kapoor. I loved all three—Dilip Kumar, Raj Kapoor and Dev Anand.

My love for Dev Anand, however, started in full earnest after I saw *Nau Do Gyarah*. The jacket I was wearing in the photo you're talking about—that material was supposed to have been made into a coat. Amma told me to go to Azaad tailor near Tasveer Mahal with the coat material. I went to the old tailor, showed him a photograph of Dev Anand in *Nau Do Gyarah*, and told him to make me a jacket just like the one the star was wearing. When Amma found out what I had done, she was furious! Amma shouted at me: 'Now what have you done?' [*both laugh*]

NMK: Did you ever tell Dev Sahib when you met him years later that you had once styled your hair like his?

JA: Yes, I did tell him and said:

> Main aap ke jaise baal banaata tha toh bahut mushkil se bante the. [I used to puff up my hair just the way you did. It was very difficult to get it right.]

Dev Anand had smiled and had replied in his inimitable style:

> Mere baal bhi bahut mushkil se bante the! [I found it very difficult too!]

NMK: When was the first time you fell in love?

JA: I was about fifteen and she was thirteen. She was a stylish and unusual girl. She wore unusual khadi prints and wore her hair in a different way from the other girls. Some years later Sadhana made that fringe popular. There was something special about her. She died not so long ago. I am not sure I would like to name her.

NMK: What did love mean to you at that age?

JA: It was impossible to resist seeing her every day. And if I didn't see her, it felt like the end of the world—a real calamity. It was the first time that I had become so obsessed. I wrote her a love letter and got a positive response. She was the first girl I ever kissed. It was all so innocent. I was very much in love.

NMK: How did your first love story end?

JA: It ended when I left Aligarh, when my father took me to Bhopal.

NMK: Before we move on, can you talk about some of your other Aligarh friends?

JA: I was very close to Farhan Mujib. We met when we were both eleven. We were classmates at Minto Circle. Farhan's mother, Jamila Mujib, was closely related to Ismat Chughtai.

Farhan Mujib was fond of the movies and, although I had already seen *Mother India,* he wanted me to see it again with him. When the song 'Pi ke ghar aaj pyaari dulhania chali' came on the screen, he got all excited seeing those wide landscape shots and bullock carts lining the horizon. That's when Farhan cried out loudly: 'Shaabaash! [Well done!]' I'll never forget that!

Though we took very different paths in life, we were always in touch. He had a beautiful singing voice and one of his favourite songs was 'Nain so nain', the duet from *Jhanak Jhanak Payal Baaje.* He was an exceptional painter, a Doctor of Education (Ph.D., University of London) and a Professor of Physics at AMU. Farhan, a connoisseur of cinema and theatre, had a delicious sense of humour. His wife, Dr Fawzia Mujib, has recently retired from AMU where she was a Reader in Physics. She is a dear friend too.

When Honey and I had a son, I named him Farhan, after my closest friend. Sadly, he passed away in 2011. He was a true Renaissance man.

NMK: I remember meeting him at your Juhu house some years ago. He was indeed a fine person.

MUZTER KHAIRABADI
(1869–1927)

Javed Akhtar's grandfather was a renowned poet celebrated for his ghazals, thumris and bhajans. He was also a judge in the state court of Gwalior.

Safia Akhtar.   Jan Nisar Akhtar.

In 1943, the poet Jan Nisar Akhtar married Safia Siraj in Lucknow. Celebrated progressive writers, both of them came from a formidable lineage of scholars and poets. A recognised author, Safia was the sister of the famous poet Majaz.

Javed Akhtar lost his mother in 1953 when he was eight years old. Seen here with his mother and brother Salman (*left*). Nainital Studio. 1950.

After his mother passed away in 1953, Javed Akhtar was brought up in Lucknow by his maternal grandparents.

(l to r) Asma, Javed, Sumbul, Salman, Urfi and Irfan, who is standing with a book in his hand. Sumbul and Irfan are his Aunt Hamida's childen and Asma and Urfi are the children of his cousin, whom he called 'Abbu Bhai', and Dulhan Bhabhi.

Aunt Hamida and her husband Abu Salim were professors of Economics. They raised Javed from the ages of 10 to 15. Seen here with their now grown children, Irfan and Sumbul. c. 1975.

Photo credit: Abu Salim

Aligarh, 1950s.

Aged 12, dressed in the style of Dev Anand, his favourite actor in childhood. The jacket he is wearing here was inspired by the star's clothes in *Nau Do Gyarah* (dir. Vijay Anand, 1957).

Bhopal. 1960s.
Aged 18, this ID card was made for the
Youth Festival, Delhi, 1963, where young
Javed participated in a group discussion. It
was at the festival that he happened to meet
Amjad Khan who was representing Bombay
University in Drama.

Bombay. 1970s.

With brother Salman Akhtar and Aunt Hamida. This photograph was taken in Delhi a few months before his aunt, whom he regarded as a second mother, passed away in August 2015.

Javed spent much of his childhood in the care of Abu Salim, Aunt Hamida's husband. He considers Abu Salim among the important influences in his life.

Shabana and Javed.

Photograph by Gautam Rajadhyaksha.

With daughter Zoya.

With son Farhan.

His maternal uncle, Majaz was a great romantic and revolutionary poet. He died at the age of 42 and is known as the Keats of Urdu poetry.

His younger maternal uncle, Ansar Harwani was a freedom fighter who spent many years imprisoned in a British jail during colonial rule. A close associate of Subhas Chandra Bose, Ansar Harwani became a Member of Parliament later in life.

The Salim-Javed years. The 1970s and '80s were dominated by the work of this talented writing duo. Their films remain a significant part of Indian cinema history, and include titles like *Zanjeer*, *Deewaar*, *Sholay*, *Trishul* and many others. They met in 1965 on the sets of *Sarhadi Lutera*. Javed Akhtar wrote some of the dialogue of *Sarhadi Lutera* and Salim Khan played the romantic lead.

With Faiz Ahmed Faiz.

With Ahmed Faraaz.

With Shivmangal Singh Suman.

With Neeraj.

With Sunil Gangopadhyay.

Javed Akhtar's ex-wife, Honey Irani, seen here with their children, Zoya and Farhan. 1970s.

With Zoya and Farhan.

Shabana and Javed.

During his school days, Javed Akhtar was a great fan of Dev Anand's. His affections switched to Dilip Kumar during his college days.

With Dilip Kumar.

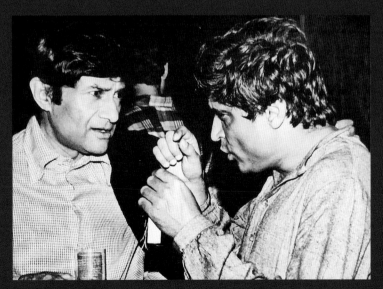

With Dev Anand. 1970s.

With granddaughter Shakya.

With granddaughter Akira.

It sounds like you had great friends in Aligarh and were living a comfortable, secure life with your uncle and aunt. So why did you want to leave?

JA: I got involved with some rough kids and some of them turned against me. They started terrorising me. I thought if I moved away from Aligarh and lived with my father in Bombay, it was a good way of escaping them.

NMK: Why were they after you? Who were they?

JA: They were a gang of delinquents from the main city; young boys between seventeen and nineteen. They were real hoodlums and carried knives and knuckle-dusters. They used to tell me to steal Amma's jewellery. I believe that somebody asked them to harass me—someone from my circle. We had this cricket club and there was some politics about who would become the Captain of the team. There was rivalry involved, if I remember rightly, and a couple of older boys—I know who they were, though I prefer not to name them because they aren't alive anymore—might have paid this gang to make my life hell.

I was living in mortal fear of these boys, though I don't know why I did not have the guts to tell my aunt and uncle about them. Instead, I told everyone I did not want to live in Aligarh anymore. Amma was not at all in favour of my leaving. When I kept insisting, my father was forced to come to Aligarh to take me away. I thought I was going to Bombay to live with him if not in the same house as him, at least in the same city, but instead we landed up in Bhopal where he left me with my stepmother's family.

Just look at my father! He knew my relationship with my stepmother was bad because one summer holiday when Salman and I had gone to Bombay for two months and stayed with them, I could sense she disliked me. She made it obvious. Yet, he leaves me with her family.

NMK: Was it because you answered her back?

JA: I don't think so, nor was I aggressive towards her. Not at all. But she was so suspicious of me, and felt I treated her like a 'step' mother. The relationship was spoilt. And here my father was taking me to Bhopal to live in her home with her parents, sisters and brothers, instead of letting me stay with him in Bombay.

Why did my father leave me with a family I didn't even know? Even though this stepchild landed at their gates uninvited, they were very nice to me, especially my stepmother's younger sister, Saeeda Apa. In her, I found a lifelong friend.

NMK: What was your father thinking by leaving you in their home?

JA: I don't know! It was the height of insensitivity. Though I must say they were good people and I got on well with them and I enjoyed living with them. Their house was called Hilal Manzil and unlike Amma's house where you could not even listen to a film song on the radio—it was considered a total no-no—here I could listen to Vividh Bharati and Radio Ceylon. I could talk about films and read film magazines.

I would be very ungrateful if I didn't mention two people who helped me emotionally and otherwise. One was Saeeda, the younger sister of my stepmother whom I have mentioned. She was about five years older than me, and I still regard her as an elder sister. Whenever I go to Bhopal, I do not leave the city without meeting her. Many have said that I can relate to people of all generations and now am very close to Saeeda's children who live in Delhi. Her daughter, Baaraan Ijlal, is emerging as an important and excellent artist. Saeeda Apa's son, Moonis, is also a highly creative and talented person.

The other person who was very good to me was Jahan Qadr Chughtai, an old friend of my father's. He was married to another of my stepmother's sisters. Since he was teaching at Saifia College in Bhopal, everyone used to call him 'Master Sahib'. I called him Chugtai Sahib.

Though I had problems with my stepmother, it is ironic that the people who were very kind to me were her close relatives.

NMK: You speak of kindness. What is your definition of a good person?

JA: It's very simple. The only criterion is how many people has that person helped without any kind of personal agenda, and without undermining their own self-respect. It is also said, to understand a person, one must live with them for fourteen years. Or travel with them. I think there's another way too, and that is seeing a person when they're very angry. All masks and inhibitions fall away—your real self, your true class emerges. And the difference between a decent and indecent person becomes obvious.

NMK: Going back to when your father took you from Aligarh from your Aunt Hamida's place to Bhopal, what did he want you to study there?

JA: I don't think he had a plan. I remember he took me to see a local Communist leader and asked him to get me admission to a university in Moscow. The man said that would not be possible. Their loss!

After living for a year in my stepmother's family home, I went to Bombay during the school summer holidays. That was a breaking point between my stepmother and me. After that, I did not return to Bombay for almost five years.

Then, one day, I was told Salman was joining me. I panicked. I had somehow managed to get by and didn't understand why my brother was coming. He had no idea how embarrassing and awkward the situation already was. My father hadn't sent me a rupee for a year, and I felt like an unwanted guest—so how could the two of us now live in my stepmother's family's home? What would I do? I panicked. After all, I was not even seventeen and had no control over events or my life. It was the kind and wonderful Chughtai Sahib who calmed me down and told me he would organise a rent-free room at Saifia College where we brothers could stay.

When I went to the station to receive Salman, I did not bring him back to Hilal Manzil; instead, I took him to a friend's house where we slept until we could move into the hostel. I wrote to my father, asking him what he was doing. I never got a reply. All these incidents added to the growing resentment and anger I felt towards him, and our relationship became increasingly negative and strained.

The room that Salman and I shared at the hostel had one chair, a small table, and no beds. We placed four classroom wooden benches side by side and put a dhurrie over them and made ourselves a sort of bed. At least we owned a dhurrie. [*laughs*]

The first few nights were impossible—we just couldn't sleep. We were scratching all night. A friend said the benches were full of bugs. The next day we put them under the hot sun, hoping to get rid of the bugs. When we came back to carry the benches to our room, there was a carpet of dead bugs lying under them. I still remember someone saying he could imagine sleeping with a few bugs but not a battalion of them!

My brother and I had very little money. We ate on credit in a restaurant called Ahad Hotel, and when we were unable to pay the bills, they refused to give us any more credit. Once again Chughtai Sahib helped us out, and we started frequenting Jameel Hotel.

Meanwhile, my interest in films was growing and, despite our meagre resources, we somehow managed to buy cinema weeklies like *Screen* and *Cine Advance*. I read up on film news and was aware of the films being made. Once we had a big bundle of magazines, we'd sell them to a raddi-wallah, and with that money we'd go and see a movie.

Salman stayed in Bhopal for a year. He did his pre-university there. I must confess I was short-tempered and nasty to him. After a year Salman went back to Amma's house in Aligarh where she and Abu Salim Sahib took care of his education. He did his MBBS there and went to Chandigarh to study further. He was an exceptional student. He got a scholarship and left for America in 1973, where he studied at Jefferson University, just outside Charlottesville, and graduated from there. Today, he's a hugely successful psychoanalyst. He gives lectures all over the world, including at Harvard. I am so proud of him. He's written almost a hundred books and is a very good Urdu poet. He writes poetry in English too. He's a talented man. If my brother had stayed on in Bhopal, he would never have achieved what he has.

NMK: Why do you feel that?

JA: In Aligarh, it was our uncle Abu Salim who told Salman: 'We will eat one roti less but we will give you the best education.' Who would have done that in Bhopal?

Life was tough for me for many years, but it was tougher for Salman. I was street-smart and a survivor. He was a sensitive and decent person, and deserved better parenting, a better father, a better brother, and a mother who did not die on him.

NMK: It sounds like you still feel guilty towards him.

JA: Yes, I do. I was working at Sippy Films and was comparatively comfortable when Salman wrote to me from Chandigarh and asked me to send him five hundred rupees. I took out five hundred rupees from the bank to send a money order but I didn't. When I think back, this is one incident I have not been able to forgive myself for. To this day I feel very guilty that I let him down and did not send those five hundred rupees.

NMK: Unlike you, did Salman have a good relationship with your father?

JA: I think it is for him to answer that. But I must tell you about two little incidents. When my half-sister Uneza was thirteen, she came to know she had another half-brother whose name was Salman. She was living with our father. That means for thirteen years Uneza did not hear Salman's name mentioned in the house.

The second incident I recall was when my father had gone to Chandigarh for a mushaira with his old friend Sahir Ludhianvi. Salman was studying at the Post Graduate Institute of Medical Education & Research in Chandigarh at the time and my brother went to meet him. Our father was quite surprised to see Salman and asked him what he was doing in Chandigarh. He was not even aware that Salman was studying there. Salman invited him to his hostel for dinner, wanting him to meet some of his friends. All the boys got together and organised a nice meal, but our father did not turn up. Not because he had fallen ill or something; instead, he clearly preferred to spend the evening with Sahir than to see his own son. Once again, Salman was left disappointed, and embarrassed in front of his friends.

NMK: Because of your difficult relationship with your father, your uncle Abu Salim with whom you lived in Aligarh must have been very important to you. Can you tell me about your uncle?

JA: When I look back, I am doubly impressed and moved by him. He was an amazing person. He was born in a small village near Azamgarh, the son of a maulvi who put his children in a madrasa to study. My uncle then went on to Aligarh University, where he met Amma. They were class fellows doing their MA in Economics and they soon fell in love. Sometime later, Abu Salim studied at the London School of Economics from where he graduated. When he returned to India, he was offered a job as a reader at AMU in the Economics department.

He was a good-looking man. Much better looking than Amma, I must say! He was a man who had a humble background and yet, he developed himself into such a sophisticated person with upper-class tastes. In some ways I think Amma held him back, otherwise he could have got even further in life. She was conservative and so careful about the lives of those dear to her that she did not want them to take any risks. Ultimately, he became a big shot in the ILO,

International Labour Organization, and worked at their African headquarters. For many years they lived out of India and when, finally, my uncle retired they settled in Delhi.

I am so grateful to him for putting up with me for all those years in Aligarh because I was a problem child. A Dennis the Menace type! I did everything a young boy should not do—I fought with people, bunked school, sometimes stole money from Amma, even though it was two or three rupees. With that money I'd buy chocolates or go to a movie. I never had the courage to steal ten rupees.

NMK: Sounds like you were wild!

JA: I was wild—and to think my uncle tolerated me at all! I was his wife's nephew, not even his own son or his sister's son. I was so unruly that I could not have a decent relationship with him. I would run away from home because I had stolen money or I had done some mischief—broken a window or something—and yet, he was so good to me. He sat me down and talked to me as if I was an adult. He tried to make me understand things, which, at the time, I did not understand. [*laughs*]

In some ways Amma was a strange person. She had a sort of sibling rivalry with my mother, who was five years older than her. Even in her nineties she would say: 'I loved my sister. Your father did not treat her well; he neglected her so much.' She also told me contradictory stories of their childhood—like when the kapre-wallah [fabric vendor] came to the house, my mother would say:

Let Hamida choose what she wants, then I'll tell you what I want. Because I know if I buy some fabric first, she will buy the same fabric.

Amma was an old lady when she recounted these stories to me and even decades later, I could see the same hurt and anger in her eyes. It never went away. I don't think she was a happy person, and I must accept that I must have added to her unhappiness. But she was a fortunate lady. She had a superb husband and lovely children. who were extremely caring towards their parents. Her son, Irfan Salim, lives in San Francisco and was featured on the cover of *Businessworld* in the US. Her daughter, Dr Sumbul Warsi, retired recently. She was a paediatrician and Medical Director at the Holy Family Hospital in Delhi. She has a very good reputation. Sumbul is like a sister to me, not a cousin. Whenever I go to Delhi, I visit her. After all, she grew up in front of me when we were all living together in Aligarh.

NMK: Sounds like you kept in close contact with your Aunt Hamida through the years.

JA: Yes, whenever I'd go to Delhi, I would meet her. Even after films like *Deewaar* and *Sholay*—I had become somewhat known—she would talk to me in the same gruff tone and say nasty things to me as she had always done. My cousin Sumbul would get embarrassed—how could her mother talk to me like that? I would tell Sumbul:

> Why are you bothered? This is strictly between my Amma and me. She has the right to say anything she wants to me.

NMK: What kind of things did she say?

JA: One of her favourite lines was:

> Agar hum nahin hote toh aaj tum sarkon pe maare-maare ghoom rahe hote. Humne tumhein bacha diya. [If I wasn't in your life, you would be roaming the streets like a pauper. I saved you.]

How could I feel offended by this old lady? I'd make light of it and answer her back jokingly:

> Ek baat kahoon aap se? Aap ke hone ke baad bhi main bahut dinon sarkon pe maara-maara ghoomta raha hoon. [Can I say something? Despite you having saved me, I still had to roam the streets like a pauper for a long time.]

NMK: Maybe she was joking with you.

JA: No, no, she was deadly serious. Amma believed it. But I know she loved me till the last day of her life. She didn't need to have loved me so much. She was known in the family for her bitter tongue, and when I was much older, I enjoyed her comments. She loved me and I loved her. She was a mother to me. If your mother has an acidic tongue, what can you do? She will always remain my mother.

But there was one overriding thing that made Amma very unhappy for many years and that was knowing that my brother Salman and I were often not on talking terms. It was on her insistence that we met in her house.

NMK: It must have been very upsetting for you to lose your aunt in 2015.

JA: I lost a mother when I was a kid, and I lost a mother when I was an adult. After Amma passed away, l developed a different kind of relationship with my uncle, Abu Salim. He outlived Amma and was staying with his daughter, Sumbul, in Delhi. I found a lot of similarities in our ways of thinking. He was a rationalist, an atheist, and a hard-core secularist.

He died a few years ago—he was over ninety. In his will he asked to be cremated and not buried. And that is what happened. It caused great unhappiness among our relatives—some of whom even refused to come to the crematorium. But Sumbul put her foot down and said she would follow his wishes no matter what.

NMK: Sounds like your uncle mattered a lot to you.

JA: I am so grateful, not only to him but also to Amma—she was bittersweet. She was nice to me and then she'd say something very nasty. Although she had an acidic way of speaking, she looked after me, and I can never forget that.

After Amma passed away, my brother Salman said: 'Let's not meet, our relationship is fake.' Maybe he was right. I believe a relationship is like a plant and if you uproot it from one pot and replant it in another pot, it will take time to take root. The plant will grow again because roots grow naturally. Salman did not give our relationship enough time and so we stopped meeting. Now, I'm willing to meet him on his terms. Because I don't want to fight with him anymore and there's no point in fighting. We're in the last lap of our lives, so I hope he meets me one day soon.

NMK: What about Zoya and Farhan? Do they get on with their uncle?

JA: They get on famously. They're very close to him. I have good relations with his children, Kabir and Nishat. Kabir is a very successful editor and director in Hollywood and has made some TV serials there. He is an Emmy Award winner, and I can see him directing a feature film someday. He's an exceptionally bright young man.

His younger sister, Nishat, is very talented too. She's a painter and draws so well. For a long time, she worked at Nike and is now the Vice-President of an advertising company. She lives in Portland and Kabir is in LA. Kabir is in his forties and Nishat must be in her late thirties. Kabir is soon getting married to a lovely girl called Charlotte.

Out of our four children, Kabir, Nishat, Zoya and Farhan, two are unmarried. I don't know if it has something to do with the first marriages of both Salman and me! [*laughs*]

NMK: Is Salman more disciplined than you?

JA: Far more! I see a lot of my brother in my son Farhan, who is very organised and disciplined. Salman is careful with money; he knows how to save—I am a spendthrift. It is said that a fool and his money part very easily; if it is true, then you can consider me a fool! Can you believe I have no idea where my bank is? I don't know how much money I have in my account either. My assistant Carrol gives me the cheques I need to sign—that's it. I have an unhealthy relationship with money. I am not trying to say, 'Wow, isn't that a great thing!' In many ways, it is irresponsible.

NMK: So, Carrol Desouza, a member of your staff, looks after your finances. She seems to manage everything in your household. I think she has worked with Shabana and you for years.

JA: As far as Carrol is concerned, I do not call her a member of my staff; she is a member of my family. In this house Carrol takes more decisions than Shabana and me put together! [*laughs*]

I must tell you about another person who has worked with me for many years. I'm talking about Haroon Sahib. We've talked about full circles; this is another full circle. When I was sleeping rough at Kamal Studios, he was the Deputy Manager there. Some years later, when he was out a job, he came to see me and from that point on, he worked with me, looking after all my affairs. Very sadly, Haroon Sahib died a few years ago.

NMK: There are other staff members who seem very much part of your world. Whenever I've visited your home over the years, those same people open doors, bring coffee and biscuits, and answer landlines.

JA: Loyalty is not a one-way street. If it's one-way, it does not last very long. All the people who work with me, like Kishore, who is my driver-cum-valet, Roshan, the cook, Rita, the maid, Shravan, who is the general help—they've all been with me for over twenty-five years, some even thirty years. Ramu, my driver, who recently passed away, had started working with me before Zoya was born. When my children grew up and became well-known personalities, they would happily drink alcohol in my presence, but not in front of Ramu! The moment he entered the room, they'd put their glasses down because he'd get upset to see them drinking alcohol. When Ramu had heart trouble, I made sure he received the best medical care available. The doctor who operated on him was the same surgeon who performed a bypass surgery on our former prime minister, Dr Manmohan Singh.

My staff knows if there's a wedding or death in their family, or they want to buy property in their village or any of their family members are unwell, they can come to me. Their medical problems and the education of their children are my responsibility. They know if they have any problems, I will stand by them. They are loyal to me, and I am loyal to them.

NMK: Can we go back to 1960–1964—to your college days in Bhopal? What happened after Salman left?

JA: I could no longer stay at the Saifia College hostel, so one friend or another offered me a place to sleep. The wonderful brothers Aijaz and Wahaj welcomed me with open arms. I had other friends who did the same, including Mushtaq Singh, Dinesh Rai, Fateh Ullah, Sagheer, and Baldev, whose pet name was 'Kaaley'—he was a Sikh boy. I never asked them for money; all the same, they discreetly gave me a new sweater or a jacket to wear in winter.

It was thanks to my time in Bhopal that I met so many generous people. It was a dress rehearsal for how tough life turned out to be, so when I was down and out in the early days in Bombay, it was not a new experience for me.

NMK: Were your Bhopal friends from different backgrounds?

JA: Some were just young guys looking for fun. Watching girls from a distance—they knew what time a particular girl came out of the college, which bus she took to go home, etc. These activities preoccupied them.

I had happy-go-lucky friends, and friends with strong political beliefs. Some were followers of the socialist Ram Manohar Lohia; others were communists and Congress loyalists.

I was even friendly with some boys from the Rashtriya Swayamsevak Sangh, and I knew the young General Secretary of the Muslim League of Madhya Pradesh. A world of difference existed between our thinking, but he and I were friends. Then there were other friends who were steeped in poetry.

A lot of my time in Bhopal was spent with friends sitting in the college canteen and talking for hours. Or sometimes, we'd chat on the steps of a nearby temple. The pujari of the temple was very kind to us and smiled at our jokes, though our conversations were always one-sided. Then we discovered the reason why he did not speak. It was because he had taken a vow of silence. The pujari knew we students were always broke, so sometimes he took me to the temple and would apply a teeka to my forehead. I'd ring the temple bell, and then he picked up a few coins lying in front of the idol and give them to me.

Even though I was a carefree lafanga type of boy, I went to the Bhopal Municipal Library at four every afternoon and read for two hours, come thunder, lightning or rain. Besides other kinds of books, I liked reading autobiographies and even read *Uneasy Lies the Head* by King Hussein of Jordan. Now, why was I interested in Jordan?

NMK: Which of your friends influenced you the most?

JA: I think it was Khusro. He was the son of the Jagirdar of Gwalior State whose title was Shri Sahib. Although Khusro was three years older, he was studying in my class because he had failed in some year.

In many ways, Khusro was the last of a generation that belonged to a particular culture and aesthetic. He had contempt for middle-class values and in this aspect, he truly was a Jagirdar and a bit of a show-off! When I look back, I do not agree with his socio-political philosophy, though I admit he influenced my sense of aesthetics. Khusro did make a big impression on me—there was much to learn from him. He was deeply interested in Roman history and was most fascinated by Cleopatra. He read as many books as he could find about her. Khusro was a voracious reader and introduced me to *The Rise and Fall of the Roman Empire* by the English historian Edward Gibbon and to Sir William Muir, the eighteenth-century author who wrote on the life of Prophet Mohammed. Muir's book is not very complimentary. He also authored *The Caliphate: Its Rise, Decline and Fall*. Even though Khusro was a believer, it intrigued me that he would read a writer like Sir William Muir, who was hardly pro-Islam or pro-Muslim. Khurso told me he believed Muir was a good source and that's what mattered to him.

NMK: What were the things he used to talk about?

JA: I remember his ideas on society They were clearly those of a jagirdar. When speaking of democracy, he said:

> Democracy? People in a democracy are not unlike jagirdars or nawabs. In what way are they different? Do they treat the ordinary man or woman in a different manner than we do? Some maharajas treat people even better than those in a democracy.

Obviously, I did not agree with him—even if some maharajahs were fair and generous and patronised the arts, you can't justify feudalism. However, whether I agreed with Khusro or not, I knew he was larger than life.

NMK: Are you still in touch with him?

JA: I called him about fifteen years ago and said I was upset to hear that he was unwell. He replied in his usual casual tone: 'I have this banal disease called cancer. You must've heard of it.' I thought, my God! I immediately told him I was coming to Bhopal to attend a function and from there, I'd come to Gwalior to see him, and in a most cheerful tone, he replied: 'You better hurry up. I don't have much time.'

I could not say goodbye to my friend Khusro because he died before I got to Bhopal. I was very sad.

NMK: Do you have many close friends today?

JA: I have very few friends who are still around from my childhood days. But I do have friends today who are great company and mean something to me. However short the list, Honey will be on it. And I must add Sultana Abdullah who is, in fact, more like a sister to me. In humour, I say: 'She's my brother and I'm her sister!'

NMK: Could we go back to the Bhopal days, what were you studying at Saifia College?

JA: English literature, political science and Urdu literature. My father was well-known in Bhopal. My college friends admired his poetry and when they found out I was his son and Majaz's nephew, they were sufficiently impressed. They might even have given me preferential treatment as a result.

NMK: Were you a good student?

JA: I was a poor student. I was not interested in textbooks. At the same time—please forgive this immodesty and you can ask any of my college friends who are still around—I was considered one of the most brilliant boys, even though I was always in the third division in both school and college.

I excelled in everything, just not in the exams. Somehow people were impressed with me because I was into debating, gymnastics, loved pranks, and remembered pages and pages of poetry by heart. If there was a Bait Baazi in Urdu—we call it Antakshari in Hindi—I'd win hands down, but I did not read my coursebooks. Before the college exams I took a few keys—there is something called 'keys'—and I prepared ten to twelve questions and that was it.

NMK: What about mathematics?

JA: That was my ultimate Waterloo. [*both laugh*]

NMK: Was there no subject you liked?

JA: History. I liked history.

My attendance in class was pathetic—a mere three per cent. To be frank with you, I could not afford to pay the college fees, so they waived the fees and allowed me to sit for the exams because I'd won trophies for the college as an ace debater. My friend Dinesh Rai, who was from a very well-respected, old Kayastha family from Bhopal, was a great debater too. When I was sixteen, I wrote a subject for the debate, which won me my first trophy—the proposition was 'Only religion can make this world a heaven'. A view I opposed in my teens and still do.

In 1963, I represented Vikram University in the National Youth Festival in a group discussion. It was during the festival that I saw a stage play that the Bombay University presented entitled 'Ae mere watan ke logon'. Amjad Khan was playing the lead. Ten years later, when *Sholay* was being cast, Salim Sahib and I recommended Amjad Khan for the role of Gabbar Singh.

NMK: How amazing!

I know that you recently found the speech, 'Only religion can make this world a heaven', thanks to another of your Bhopal friends, Mushtaq Singh.

JA: Yes, it's entirely thanks to Mushtaq Singh. He is a Sardar and a very close friend of mine and in fact he gave me the kara, which I still wear on my right wrist. He is a few years older than me. Over time, we lost touch since he kept moving from country to country.

Sometime in 2018, Shabana and I had gone to London, and I was interviewed by the BBC to comment on a book of poetry. I went through the pages of the book and decided to read the preface. To my surprise, the name of the preface writer was Mushtaq Singh. I asked the BBC journalist if this Mr Singh had ever lived in Bhopal and the journalist said: 'Oh yes, he has mentioned Bhopal several times.' I asked for his number and the journalist said he did not have it and would call me that evening with it, which he did. I took a chance and called. I said: 'Mushtaq, this is Javed.' He immediately recognised my voice and sounding thrilled, he said:

Arey tum kahaan ho? Mera number kaise mila? [Where are you? How did you get my number?]

I explained how and, excitedly, we fixed to meet the next day. He came and we hugged. We had tears in our eyes as we talked about the old days. Fifty-four years had passed since we had met—1964–2018. Then, casually, he said he had an envelope with some papers that I had left behind in the room he generously let me share when I had no place to sleep. During the coldest nights in winter, we had to share the same bed because he had only one blanket. He also had some clothes stitched for me as I did not have any decent clothes to wear.

Mushtaq Singh carried that envelope with him from Bhopal to Glasgow, Glasgow to Sydney and then finally from Sydney to London, where he had settled down. He asked me to pick up my papers the next day. I said I was leaving London, and that you would call and collect the envelope for me before you travelled to Bombay.

Thanks to Mushtaq Singh, I got back my lost treasure. You will remember that I could not hold back my tears when I saw that handwritten speech, 'Only religion can make this world a heaven', written when I was sixteen, and that old autograph book of mine.

You may not believe I was an avid autograph hunter, but I was! The craze lasted from the age of ten to about sixteen. I managed to collect the signatures of many leading film personalities, writers, singers, sportsmen and even Pandit Jawaharlal Nehru.

NMK: Where did you see Pandit Nehru?

JA: Pandit-ji was coming to Aligarh to lay the foundation of the Maulana Azad Library. From Minto Circle, a group of students, including my friend Farhan Mujib and I, plus students from Abdullah Girls' College, were chosen to form a huge choir and sing for the visiting dignitaries. The choir had to get to the stage through the VIP entrance, so when the programme was over, and because I had access to the VIP exit, I ran after Pandit-ji just as he was sitting in a car with the Vice-Chancellor of AMU, Dr Zakir Husain.

Can you imagine being able to get so close to a prime minister today, let alone pushing an autograph book through his car window? Pandit-ji looked at the sketches of himself and the Tiranga, which were made by my childhood friend Hajra Zuberi. When he saw the drawings, he must have assumed I had laboured hard over them, so I probably merited an autograph! He signed a short version of his name 'JL Nehru', and they drove away. I think two things helped me to get that autograph—my audacity and Hajra's sketches.

At the end of the day, getting back my lost treasure is all thanks to Mushtaq Singh. I'm so grateful to him for restoring some of the past to me.

NMK: It shows how much he valued your friendship. And you his. You still wear the kara he gave you and he kept your papers. Did you ever see Pandit Nehru again?

JA: In 1963, when I was at the Youth Festival, all the boys and girls were invited to his house on his birthday, 14 November. Believe me, there was no checking, no security, no metal detectors—nothing! We students formed a queue and made our way into the huge garden which was behind the house. Pandit-ji came and met us all. I was a bit fearless and went up to him and shook his hand and said: 'Happy birthday to you, sir.' I still remember the feel of his hand—he had a very soft hand. That was his last birthday because he passed away the next year on 27 May 1964.

NMK: This autograph book of yours—I am curious to know how you managed to get so many celebrities to sign. I looked through the book and found the range of stars and personalities most impressive. You got the signatures of Kishore Kumar, Madhubala, Waheeda Rehman, and many others.

JA: I'm talking about 1961. It was the year I visited my father in Bombay. Since I collected autographs, I was keen to attend *Filmfare*'s annual awards night because I knew there'd be many stars there. My father, as I've mentioned, was a close friend of Sahir Ludhianvi's, but neither Sahir Sahib nor my father were invited. The actor Bharat Bhushan was a friend of theirs and he had received an invite. He was born in Meerut and educated in Aligarh and spoke beautiful Urdu. It was a big deal to get invited to the *Filmfare* awards ceremony in those days. So, my father asked Bharat Bhushan's secretary, Mr Parashar, to get me an invitation. By the way, Mr Parashar's nephew is the well-known director, Pankaj Parashar.

That year, the event took place at the Birla Matushri Hall on Marine Lines. Dilip Kumar had won the Best Actor Award for *Kohinoor,* though he did not attend the ceremony. Bina Rai won the Best Actress Award for *Ghunghat,* and she went on to the stage to receive her award. Armed with my autograph book, I made my way through the crowd of stars and got many signatures.

In those days you could smoke anywhere and when the invitees started leaving the auditorium as the function ended, I saw Bimal Roy standing near the stage. He had just won the Best Director Award for *Parakh.* He was about to light a cigarette when I ran over to him and asked for his autograph. He threw away his unlit cigarette and signed my book. That was my only encounter with this great film director. Then I saw Nimmi-ji exiting the hall and ran after her. She smiled at me very sweetly and said: 'I am in a great hurry. I will give you my autograph some other day.'

That 'some other day' came fifty-eight years later. Sometime at the end of 2019, I got a call saying Nimmi-ji wants to talk to you. I had no idea whether she was even alive. I immediately took the call, and she told me some guests of hers were visiting Bombay and they wanted to meet me. I went over to her place, met her friends, and took out my autograph book. I said:

This is the autograph book which fifty-eight years ago you had refused to sign. May I ask for your autograph now?

Nimmi-ji gave me a big smile and signed my book. A few months later, in March 2020, I heard that she had passed away.

NMK: She acted in some very interesting films and had a graceful presence and a nice voice. I especially liked her in Mehboob Khan's *Amar* and *Aan*.

You were aware of all the early actors, so films must have been important to you when you were growing up.

JA: To be honest, it was books first. Films were not part of our everyday home life. They came later. In 1963, I remember seeing Nasir Hussain's *Jab Pyaar Kisise Hota Hai* at least three times at Bhopal Talkies. And to think, years later, I would be co-writing *Yaadon ki Baraat* for Nasir Sahib!

I was seven when I saw a film that made a great impact on me and that was Mehboob Khan's *Aan*. It was one of the early Indian films in colour and Dilip Kumar played this swashbuckling handsome young man. In one scene, he sings, 'Dil mein chhupa ke pyaar ka toofaan le chale ...' while driving a horse-drawn carriage—clip-clop, clip-clop—there was Nadira, who played the arrogant princess sulking in the rear seat behind him. The way Dilip Kumar delivered his dialogue ... he was *the* hero for me.

NMK: You must have been thrilled to meet him when you did. Where did you meet him for the first time?

JA: At the Bandra Gymkhana. He was playing badminton and I had gone there with Salim Sahib, who knew him. I thought: 'Oh, goodness me, here's Dilip Kumar!' I tried to keep my dignity when I shook his hand, though my eyes were twitching, and they didn't stop twitching for hours. [*both laugh*]

Some years later, Dilip Sahib and I spent a lot of time together. We used to often meet and have drunk several nights away. He was not just an exceptional actor; he was the symbol of a certain culture and gravitas which is lost today.

NMK: You have a thousand stories in you. If you were to give the go-ahead for a biography, who would you choose to write it?

JA: Have I not chosen someone? What are you doing, Munni?

NMK: Ours is a conversational biography, Javed Sahib. I'm thinking about an autobiography that you might write one day.

JA: I prefer the idea of a memoir, to write about specific events. I think talking about I, me, myself, is not important. If you reflect on life and find insights into why you did certain things—that's worth talking about.

NMK: When I ask film practitioners about whether they would write an autobiography, they often give the same answer: 'We can't tell the truth because it might hurt too many people, so it's better not to write at all.'

Do you think people in India avoid autobiographies for fear of offending others?

JA: It's easy to judge people, but we must put ourselves in their shoes. If someone writes about an extramarital affair, for example, it may be damaging, because today the person they're talking about could be married with children or grandchildren and have a certain image in society. Or suppose someone behaved in a petty way towards you, and time has passed, should you dig up old bitter feelings—dig up those graves and find skeletons? Should you do that? There is no one in the world who has not made serious mistakes in their lives. How to own up to this? How to take responsibility? And when?

The two biographies I have personally liked, one is Mahatma Gandhi's—I think he has spoken so truthfully about himself. Objectivity of that kind is difficult and inconvenient. I don't think most people have the guts to write as honestly. Then there's Maxim Gorky's *My Childhood, In the World* and *My Universities*. They are brilliant books. I was only thirteen when I first read Gorky's novel, *Mother*, and later I read his *Tales of Italy*.

NMK: What about the Urdu poets? Are there many autobiographies in Urdu?

JA: There is Josh Malihabadi's *Yaadon ki Baraat*—it's not exactly an autobiography, it's more of a memoir. Manto did not write an autobiography, although he has written several articles about his work and has talked about his life. The great Urdu writer Qurratulain Hyder has written a fascinating autobiography titled *Kaar-e Jahan Daraz Hai*. It's such a fine portrait of a family.

I've mentioned Sabir Dutt to you. He was a distant cousin of Sunil Dutt's and a close confidant of Sahir Sahib. He used to live in Sahir Sahib's house and looked after his affairs. In Sabir Dutt's magazine *Fann aur Shaksiyat* [Art and Personality], he has highlighted the work of several authors. He had also edited a special issue entitled: 'Aap-beeti Number' [autobiography/in first person] that featured some 150 writers and poets writing about their lives in ten or fifteen pages. Obviously, they are not complete autobiographies, but they are first-person accounts.

My pyschoanalyst brother Salman once commented something on the lines of 'When you read those accounts, you realise that everybody was wronged at some point in their lives. Now, if everybody was wronged, then who was doing wrong to them? If everybody is a victim, then who is the victimiser? The fact is each one of us is a victim and a victimiser.'

NMK: That's an interesting thought.

JA: Sometimes, I wonder how thoughts are formed in our brain. Some people believe that ideas and thoughts are sent to us by an unknown force, then why don't they come to us in Latin or Chinese? Such esoteric ideas are nothing but superstition. I believe when our conscious, pre-conscious and subconscious mind work together, a new idea takes birth, which takes even us by surprise.

I think the mind is one big house. Our immediate memory and

thoughts—the conscious mind is like the drawing room or perhaps an office, while we have other rooms, attics, basements and bedrooms, and even empty rooms. Maybe even a library.

NMK: Carl Jung wrote something to the effect that the psyche was made up of many interacting systems—something like the rooms in the mind that you speak of.

JA: I hope he did not also say there's a no man's land between our conscious and subconscious mind. [*smiles*]

The conscious mind does not always help us when we're creating something. When I'm writing a song, I listen to the tune many times and go to sleep for an hour or so. I find the song words come to me more easily when I wake up. I have renewed energy because my unconscious mind has been allowed to work.

Poetry or any creative act takes place in this no man's land between our conscious and subconscious mind. All art is a paradox. Art means getting lost in your imagination and emotions, but you need craft along with those instincts. Craft means being objective, judicious, and sometimes even manipulative. All these things happen simultaneously. I'll borrow Ghalib's words to describe what I think you need to create art:

Saadgi-o purkaari bekhudi-o-hushyaari
[Simplicity, intricacy, forgetfulness, awareness]

NMK: Besides Ghalib, who are the writers you most admire?

JA: I'm very impressed with the work of Krishan Chander, Qurratulain Hyder, Ismat Chughtai, Manto and the Marathi playwriter Vijay Tendulkar. They were undoubtedly amazing writers. The books of Dostoevsky, Tolstoy, Balzac, and in non-fiction, Richard Dawkins and Yuval Noah Harari are also great. I loved *Oliver Twist* by Dickens and admired the work of Oscar Wilde and George Bernard Shaw. I have a special place in my heart for Victor Hugo. Besides a formidable talent, he was the first author to fight for the copyright of writers.

I told you how it was thanks to Amma that I came to hear of Krishan Chander in my childhood. When I grew older, I became a big fan of his. At seventeen or eighteen, there were three people in this country whom I admired the most: Pandit Jawaharlal Nehru, Krishan Chander and Dilip Kumar.

Years later, I even told Krishan Chander and Dilip Kumar about this. I have a photograph of the three of us sitting together. I was very fortunate to have developed personal relations with Krishan Chander. I spent hours with him and have even read some of his manuscripts. I noticed there was not a single word struck through or replaced by the author in some seventy or eighty pages. It's remarkable.

He was a very shy and reticent person in personal life. You could never guess that here was a man who could write in such a romantic and passionate manner and with such an easy flow, poetic expressions and great wit. You never felt that if you met him. He could not speak three sentences in flow—he stammered, left a sentence midway and started another. He was a bit awkward, but undoubtedly a giant of a writer.

NMK: What did you like about his work?

JA: I liked his tremendous sensitivity. His ideology was so progressive, his diction was magical. Ali Sardar Jafri once said that Krishan Chander was a dishonest poet who was hiding in a crowd of prose writers.

NMK: That's a lovely description. Who were the other writers you got to know?

JA: I knew Ismat Chughtai and Qurratulain Hyder well. They had very different personalities. The vivacious Ismat Chughtai was my mother's very dear friend. We were like family and whenever we came to Bombay, we stayed in her flat. She lived on the first floor of Indus Court on A Road, Churchgate, bang opposite Jai Hind College.

Everyone called her 'Ismat Apa'. She was witty and intelligent with a sharp insight. She was a grounded lady with impeccable values—a true feminist. She has been translated into English and other languages. Her greatness is now dawning on people. The kind of progressive thinking this woman had in her time was astounding. Her heroines are not perfect people. They are liars, cheats, two-timers, they'd sleep around, even steal, but you fell in love with those women. They were no devis and Madonnas in her stories. They were real people with an ordinary sense of morality. Yet you could tell the core of her characters was different and worth respecting, which is a great achievement. Ismat Chughtai never sympathised with her characters. Perhaps, she believed sympathising is deliberately humiliating a human being. Her writing touches your heart.

Her conversations, her short stories and novels were not different from the person she was. She talked the way she wrote and wrote the way she talked. She was the opposite of Krishan Chander. Ismat Chughtai rejected the idea that there was a planned thought or craft behind her prose. She did not take herself too seriously and would brush off any questions about her writing technique or her craft.

When I was fifty years old and an established writer in the film industry, Jai Hind College asked me to give a speech to their students at their annual function. I told them that just across this narrow road, opposite your gate, there's a building called Indus Court, and I used to come there when I was five years old. It has taken me forty-five years to cross this road!

NMK: What about Qurratulain Hyder?

JA: Her friends called her 'Ainee Apa'. She was a monumental writer. It's a pity that the world does not know her. She has written some very good novels. Her *Aag ka Darya* [River of Fire] can be compared to the world's great epic novels. The book was released when she was thirty or thirty-one. What a novel! The story starts from the Gupta period and ends at the Partition of India. It moves through different periods, and not only centres on characters but also includes a look at the philosophy, the beliefs and the rituals in different periods of history. She has captured the culture of 2,000 years in *Aag ka Darya*. She was a great writer.

She also wrote a novella about the Urdu–Parsi theatre through the life of an actress and how the Urdu–Parsi theatre gradually evolved into early cinema. She describes the changing feudal times and how democracy was coming and how those feudal leaders, the nawabs and rajas, became political leaders. Amazing story! Her way of writing was first mastering the topic through rigorous research and collecting material from many libraries and many sources. When I visited her home, I saw she had amassed pamphlets, posters and scripts of those Urdu–Parsi plays.

NMK: What was title of this short story? It sounds fascinating.

JA: *Dilruba.* It's about four generations of feudal lords and four generations of theatre actresses. You have the rise of the actress as she becomes a big movie star on the one hand, and the decline of the feudal lords on the other.

NMK: What about the other Urdu writers you liked?

JA: Ali Sardar Jafri analysed poetry very well. He could discuss the good and the not-so-good in poetry and why a writer had a particular kind of language. Jafri Sahib talked about the craft of writing in a way that many poets were unable to do.

I was lucky to have personally met so many writers, and that too at a very impressionable age. Take Sahir, for example. He had a fascinating personality. There was also Kaifi Azmi—he was born in a small village in a conservative Muslim Shia family and grew as a person, achieving much more than many of his highly educated colleagues. He was a farsighted man. It was a pleasure spending time with him. Sajjad Zaheer was so well-informed. Premchand's work is deeply moving, and his writing is in the realm of greatness. He is considered the father of Hindi and Urdu novels and short stories. Like Pearl S. Buck, I believe Premchand should have been awarded the Nobel Prize for Literature, especially for his *Godaan*.

NMK: You've met so many major writers. Did you ever discuss their work with them?

JA: Sometimes, I feel all creative work is an exercise in schizophrenia. On the one hand, you need fantasy, imagination, emotion, passion, forgetfulness and involvement. On the other hand, every art has a craft. And that craft is clever, calculating and surgical. They are seemingly incompatible things, yet they function in tandem in a creative person's mind.

If an actor is playing Hamlet, he can only play Hamlet if he believes he is the Prince of Denmark. The director gives him a chalk mark on the stage and wants him to say the lines 'To be or not to be, that is the question' at a certain spot on the stage where the light will fall on the actor. The actor may be convinced that he is the Prince of Denmark, and if he is that convinced, how will he remember the chalk mark? If he concentrates on finding the chalk mark, will he still believe he is the Prince of Denmark? He will have to do both things simultaneously.

It is the same with writers. Imagination, fantasy, emotion, passion stir in the writer's mind, yet there is also craft that will say—no, this paragraph is too long, this sentence is meandering, edit it, use that word instead of this. The process is surgical, clever, manipulative and objective.

In my experience, writers don't like talking about their technique. Not that it's a trade secret, they just don't wish to reveal it to themselves either. They don't want to bring it to their conscious mind or be too aware of it because it will impact their imagination and passion. I understand why they prefer to be vague, even to themselves.

NMK: Whose work do you like among the Hindi writers?

JA: Harivansh Rai Bachchan and Neeraj are among my favourite Hindi poets. There was also Shivmangal Singh Suman, a hugely important kavi [poet]. By the way, Suman-ji was my father's colleague at Victoria College in Gwalior. Among the contemporary poets, my favourite is Suryabhanu Gupt. He has a unique voice and admirable individuality.

NMK: You mentioned briefly that your father taught the former prime minister, Mr Atal Bihari Vajpayee, when he was at Victoria College.

JA: Yes, but I found out about that much later. In 1977–1978, I got a message saying that Vajpayee-ji, who was the Minister for Foreign Affairs in Mr Morarji Desai's government at that time, had come to Bombay and wanted to meet me. He was staying at Raj Bhavan. I was very engrossed with my career and was largely an apolitical person then—even the Emergency came and went and did not make much impact on me. I was what you call 'a frog in a well'. You can imagine how taken aback I was when I heard Mr Atal Bihari Vajpayee wanted to meet me.

When we met at Raj Bhavan, he introduced me to Mrs Kaul, the head of his adopted family. I later met Mrs Kaul's children. They have always lived with Vajpayee-ji and were regarded as family by him. Mrs Kaul's daughter, Gunnu-ji, was the person who lit the fire at Vajpayee-ji's cremation. They were that close.

Mrs Kaul had tears in her eyes when she told me that Vajpayee-ji and she were my father's students at Victoria College—now it's called Lakshmibai College. She spoke of being good friends with my parents and said my mother was very fond of her, and as a young student she even babysat me when my mother needed to go out. I was unaware of all this because my father had never mentioned her.

I could feel Mrs Kaul's emotion when recounting the past. People often hide their emotions, but she did not. Shabana and I formed a kind of a relationship with Vajpayee-ji. When he became prime minster, we continued to visit them occasionally and were always treated like special guests. We still have that kind of relationship with Gunnu-ji, his adopted daughter.

NMK: There are so many demands on your time, so many people in your life. Your house is always busy; unexpected visitors drop in; you get endless phone calls and text messages. I wonder how you manage to tear yourself away from everything and sit down to write.

JA: All that is true, though I do make time to write. But sitting down and writing has always been difficult for me. If I can delay that moment, I will taalo it [put it off] for another day. You feel slightly incompetent every time you try to write. Sometimes, you don't believe you can make a breakthrough. Once you have overcome the first hurdle and you find yourself in that space, gradually words come to you. Thoughts come to you that may take even you by surprise. Writing is a great pleasure then.

NMK: Do you experience the same hesitation whether writing a poem or a script?

JA: It's the same for all forms of writing—though the time needed is different. When you're writing a couplet, you're thinking of one line at a time. When it comes to writing a script, you write it over a longer span of time.

A writer is like a safe breaker. He doesn't have the key to the safe. So, he wiggles the keyhole with a pin or a bit of wire. With a lot of wiggling and patience he manages to get one lever to fall, then another and gradually the safe opens. Then words start flowing. That's how it goes.

NMK: Is the hesitation what's called a writer's block?

JA: Sometimes the very idea that there's a block creates a block. That happens too and it can make you panic. I've experienced it many times, especially in my thirties, which were supposedly the peak years of our scriptwriting. There have been many times when I've asked myself if I am capable of writing at all. They're paying me and they don't know I've exhausted myself. They think I'm a great writer, but they don't know I'm a fraud. I have nothing more to offer. This has happened to me and in those moments, I fantasised about running away to another city, changing my name and living incognito. [*both laugh*]

NMK: How did you stop yourself?

JA: Something would happen, and I'd get an idea. Even the physical process of writing is important. I write dialogue in Urdu and the descriptions in English, in longhand. I don't use a laptop. For me writing must happen between pen and paper. It's a private relationship. You may have an idea floating in your mind, but certain things only come alive when you're physically writing. Sometimes, I hear a remark that helps my mind get back into gear. The moment you get a thought and if you stay with it, ideas slowly evolve. That's how those fantasies of my running away wore off.

NMK: Do bad reviews of your poetry or a film you've scripted affect you?

JA: I honestly try to understand whether the criticism is well-founded. I may not admit it openly but in my heart of hearts I take note. If the criticism is right and if I can correct something, I will. Reviews can be biased or prejudiced. If they like you, they praise you; if they don't like you, they don't praise you or your work.

NMK: Was there a moment in your life that brought about the biggest change?

JA: I think the major event that changed my personality, my relationships, my position in society and my sense of discipline—I should say in every aspect of my life—took place on 31 July 1991 when I decided I'd never drink alcohol again. That changed my world. That made me, shall I say, very sober? [*laughs*]

In all seriousness, when I quit drinking, I became more objective. I tried to analyse my mistakes and tried to correct them. I don't know how far I've succeeded, though I have tried. I don't think I could have done what I've managed to do since 1991 if I had continued drinking, whether it was writing poetry or fighting for changes in the Copyright Bill. If I was still heavily drinking the way I used to, do you think I could have managed all that? My personal relationships improved too. And I doubt very much that I could have written the poetry I'm writing today if I had carried on drinking.

NMK: Why do you think you were drinking heavily?

JA: My drinking was based on misguided values. I thought there was something glamorous about it. Maybe it was the stories I heard about some famous Urdu poets, or the image of Devdas and the many screen versions of him that made an impact on my thinking. But drinking gradually became an addiction. When I got drunk, I often picked a fight, became unpleasant. I was nasty and aggressive to people—is that romantic or glamorous? What's romantic about it? Nothing. In part, I drank because I thought: 'After all I'm an artist, part of a lineage of poets, a carefree person.' But drinking only gave that bitter and angry person inside of me licence to emerge. It was a bad combination.

NMK: Why did alcohol change you so much?

JA: On the one hand, I had the refined culture of Lucknow ingrained in me—that I should be polite, I shouldn't say this, I shouldn't say that. I must be well-mannered. On the other hand, there was an unresolved, angry person in me because of my complicated childhood and adolescence. Tehzeeb suppressed much bitterness in me. It was a burden. I did not realise I had been troubled for a long time and so I drank like a fish. It was a problem, not only for me but for others too. It took me a long time to realise that I was making a fool of myself. So, I stopped drinking. And when I was sober, I had no choice, I had to introspect. There was no place to hide. It's so easy and comforting to believe the world has wronged you—and you're the sad victim. It's the most reassuring feeling. And to finally understand that I have victimised others and behaved in an unjust and indecent way—that was a terrible realisation.

Maybe I would have been a better husband, a better father, if I had not been drinking. Believe me, I'm not happy admitting all this, and sometimes it's difficult for me to imagine I could have been so insensitive. I could not see what the others were going through. Why couldn't I? Was I too self-obsessed? I don't know. I carry a cross of guilt on my shoulders. I know I can't undo those years, though I can try to compensate the people for the wrongs I caused. The guilt won't go away, and I'm destined to live with it.

NMK: How long were you drinking?

JA: Over two decades. I stopped in my mid-forties.

NMK: That was the time when you were very creative, writing all those hugely popular screenplays with Salim Khan.

JA: I had stopped drinking for a year. In that year, stone-sober, I wrote the dialogue of *Sholay* and *Deewaar*. But, yes, Salim Sahib and I did the writing while we were consuming a lot of alcohol. Remember we were a lot younger then.

NMK: What made you say, 'I must stop'?

JA: It didn't happen overnight. I was toying with the idea of quitting. The real reason I stopped was a selfish one. Common sense told me: 'Look, I'm in my forties, either I keep drinking and die in my mid-fifties, or if I want to live longer, I must stop.' It wasn't guilt or any great moment of enlightenment, it was my desire to live a long life.

NMK: How badly was alcohol affecting your health?

JA: That was just the problem. I was fine. It wasn't my physical health that was the issue.

In 1993, I quit smoking too. At that time, I complained to our family doctor, Dr Agarwal, of breathlessness. He got worried and asked me to see a cardiologist. This was two years after I had stopped drinking. Shabana and I went to see a cardiologist and as we were sitting in the waiting room, I told Shabana no matter what the doctors tell me after the tests are done, he is bound to say I must quit smoking. I didn't want to quit because someone else had told me to, and the only way I could quit was if I made up my mind to stop. I had a packet of Dunhills with three cigarettes left. I threw the packet away in that waiting room and said to myself: 'Now, I'm ready to see the doctor.'

The cardiologist did various tests and told me my diaphragm was not moving properly and that's why I was becoming breathless. Thankfully there was nothing wrong with my heart, though the doctor advised me:

> You're not getting any younger. You don't have any heart problems today but tomorrow you may. This is the age when people develop heart problems. You should stop smoking.

I told him I had already quit and since that day I have never smoked again.

NMK: That was disciplined of you!

JA: It's the love of life, my dear! I want to live. To me life is like reading an extremely interesting novel. I want to witness everything that happens in the world. All the major events and future discoveries. We have seen the automobile, the airplane, radio, television, and so many new inventions in the last 200 years. This is the time to live and watch.

Suppose I had died twenty-five years ago, I would not have seen the arrival of computers or mobile phone. I would not know about the internet, Google, Amazon Prime and Netflix. Imagine the things that will be invented in the next few decades. People are doing fantastic research on the functioning of the brain. There's stem cell therapy, and so many extraordinary things are being discovered, especially in medicine and space exploration. The story of life is so interesting that if you were to tell me the last chapter was missing in the book that I'm reading, I will be most dejected. To think I will not be around to see what happens next—that's what I dislike about death. [*laughs*]

NMK: Do you have many regrets? I'm not referring to the time you were drinking, I am thinking about things you might have done differently.

JA: Oh, I would have done many things differently. I wasted a lot of time in my life. If I was more mature, I believe my marriage with Honey Irani would have been different too.

Instead of going to parties and wasting time, I could have learnt another language or how to play a musical instrument. I think I have some musical talent. Some of the music directors I work with refuse to believe that I have not learnt music formally. Circumstances didn't allow me to learn music when I was young, but when I was working at Sippy Films, and we were financially secure, I could have learnt then. Right?

NMK: I'm amazed to hear you say that. I don't think you have wasted time. Even when you had no money as a young man, you told me you learnt ballroom dancing, you wrote screenplays, poetry, songs … I think you've packed ten lives into one!

You've done so much in your life, I wonder what will remain.

JA: It's your work that's remembered. People talk about Van Gogh, Shakespeare, Ghalib, Kalidas and Michelangelo—it's their work they think of. There were many others living in their era who were probably better human beings than they were, but they've been forgotten. Who knows if Shakespeare was a good person or not? Was he short-tempered or patient? Who really cares? Shakespeare is his plays; Keats is his poetry; Kurosawa is his films. If your work survives, you survive.

NMK: What do you want to be remembered for? Your work, your wit, your insightful conversations, your poetry, your unique world view or ...

JA: How does it matter if I'm not around? [*laughs*]

On a more serious note, no one is remembered for very long. If your work has lasting value, people will talk about you. Life carries on. Maybe I will be remembered for some of my poetry. People who know me personally might remember me for some of my ideas or my sense of humour. When you die, people think of you like a film they saw in their childhood. [*long pause*]

NMK: Can we go back to the time you first came in Bombay to settle down here? I remember you once told me you arrived on 4 October 1964. You were nineteen years old and that's when you began looking for work in films. What drew you to films?

JA: There was no shame for a writer to work in films because almost all the important poets and prose writers were working in the film industry at that time; they were either writing dialogue, screenplays or songs.

Don't forget, my father was already working in films as a songwriter. He had not reached the position of Sahir, Shailendra or Majrooh Sultanpuri, although he was doing well. I must admit I did not try to get into films because of those great writers—frankly, I came to Bombay because Dilip Kumar, Dev Anand, Raj Kapoor and directors like Guru Dutt, Mehboob Khan, Bimal Roy and K. Asif were working in films. I thought the film industry was glamorous and I was seduced by the world of Hindi cinema and I wanted to be a director.

At nineteen, one does not always have a clear plan. The only thing I was certain about was wanting the dialogue writer Akhtar-ul Iman to write the dialogue for my first film. He was a well-known Urdu poet and wrote excellent dialogue for many films, including B.R. Chopra's courtroom drama *Kanoon*. It was a film without songs, which is still a rarity in Indian cinema. His lines for Nana Palsikar's character in *Kanoon* were sharp and incisive.

Akhtar-ul Iman also wrote superb dialogue for Yash Chopra's *Dharmputra* and *Waqt*. He won the *Filmfare* Award for Best Dialogue for both these films. His *Flat No. 9* was disappointing and not up to his usual standard, but I made it a point to see all the films with his dialogue.

NMK: When you came to Bombay, you said you stayed with your father for only five days. Why only five days?

JA: In a fit of temper my stepmother slapped me and threw me out of the house. This happened in my father's presence. She just didn't want me around. And there I was, not even twenty years old, on the streets of Bombay with 27 naya paisa in my pocket.

NMK: Didn't your father defend you?

JA: No. There's no point talking about it now—what's done is done. I was accustomed to living a paradoxical life for years.

Whenever I had to go hungry because I didn't have a rupee to my name, I would dream of daal-chawal [lentils and rice]. In my mind's eye, I'd see steam rising from the hot daal and marvel at the whiteness of rice. Why daal-rice? Was it my favourite dish from childhood? After many years, I understood why. When you have an empty stomach for more than thirty-six hours, you can have a lot of acidity, and so your body cannot cope with spices and wants plain and simple food. And that is why your mind fantasises about daal and rice.

NMK: Besides sleeping hungry on some nights, you once told me you slept in a railway station. Is that right?

JA: Yes, I did sleep a few nights under the porch of the Khar railway station. If I had nowhere to sleep, I slept in parks and on pavements. Though, for the most part, I was welcomed in their homes by my many friends, including Javed Mahmood and his sister Zohra Jamal. Zohra Jamal was a short-story writer and a former student of my mother's. After spending some weeks with them, my friend Parvez, who was a film publicist, and another friend, Kamal Anand, and I shared a room costing ninety rupees a month. We paid thirty rupees each. Parvez is no more now, but I am still in touch with his wife. Her name is Shibani, and at that time she was his girlfriend. Her sister's name was Nazar. I used to call them 'Chhoti behen' and 'Badi behen' because the maid who came to clean their house called them by those names.

Even today, I have Shibani's number in my contacts under the name 'Chhoti behen'. We became friends. They belonged to an upper-middle-class family and generously took me to the movies and insisted I eat with them, so every night I landed up in their home. Shibani and Nazar often asked me to accompany them to fancy parties, some hosted by big industrialists, including the owner of Himalaya Bouquet. He had a huge bungalow in Powai that had a plaque on the gate that I will never forget: 'We may be vegetarian, but our dogs are not.' [*both laugh*]

At these parties, I made my presence felt by cracking jokes and telling stories. People seemed to enjoy my company. That was a plus point.

NMK: I can sense how moved you are by the kindness of your friends and strangers. I believe it was thanks to some friends you even learnt ballroom dancing.

JA: Yes. We had a common friend, Kishan Tinani. He was a few years older than me, and he was a dancer, so Shibani, Nazar and Parvez asked him to teach us ballroom dancing. That's how I came to learn it.

NMK: Were you a good dancer?

JA: I don't claim to have been exceptional. I was pretty good. I have a sense of rhythm and was graceful enough. My favourite dance was the Cha-Cha-Cha. It was crazy—I was without a job, without money to pay the rent, and yet I was learning ballroom dancing and attending fancy parties, thanks to my friends.

There are good people in this world. It is not made up of only bad people who want to harm or hurt you. If life has dealt you bad cards, sorry, tough luck!

NMK: I'm amazed you managed to retain your sense of humour.

JA: Maybe it's because of those days that I have it at all! Shock absorbers in a car are not for smooth roads but for bumpy ones, for roads with potholes. A sense of humour is a kind of shock absorber. It is meant for bad times and comes in handy for making horrid moments tolerable.

NMK: When you first started looking for work in 1964, did you introduce yourself to film producers as Jan Nisar Akhtar's son?

JA: No, I didn't. Some months after arriving here, I got a job earning fifty rupees a month as an apprentice in Mahal Pictures, Kamal Amrohi's company. That was the time when Parvez and Kamal Anand and I were sharing a room in Chuim Village in Bandra. The house belonged to the Fernandes family. Next to their kitchen they had a small room and that's where we stayed.

I must tell you about how certain inhibitions enter your psyche without you being aware. The first time in my life that I saw a dish made with pork was in the Fernandes home. When I looked at it, I felt some hesitation and fear. I decided my reaction was based on conditioning, and I did not allow myself to accept this conditioning. So, I ate some pork. I immediately felt a kind of resistance within me—what am I doing eating pork? Then, I decided if I claim to be a rationalist, I had to get rid of these feelings. Even at that age, I knew a pure rationalist would dismiss any illogical resistance.

NMK: How long were you living in Chuim Village?

JA: It wasn't long before I had to go back to Kamal Amrohi Studio and sleep in various parts of the studio compound once again, because even paying my share of thirty rupees' rent became tough. I was only earning fifty rupees at Mahal Pictures.

NMK: What films were you working on as an intern?

JA: There was *Aakhri Din Pehli Raat* by writer-director Madhusudan, though the film was shelved halfway. I also worked on *Shankar Hussain*, which was going to be directed by Kamal Amrohi Sahib himself. The original cast had Sanjeev Kumar and Feroz Khan.

Coincidentally, the first day I went to work, Kamal Amrohi was filming the screen test of a hopeful actor and it happened to be none other than Sanjeev Kumar. After the screen test was over, Sanjeev and I took the train from Andheri East; I got off at Bandra and he went on to Grant Road. We were both travelling in a third-class train compartment. At that time, neither of us could have guessed that I'd be co-writing films in which he would star.

Shankar Hussain was stalled for some reason and many years later, it was made by another director with a new cast. The film was released in 1977. When the initial filming stopped, Kamal Amrohi said he could no longer pay everyone, so that was the end of my fifty-rupee salary! [*laughs*]

At that time, I fortunately bumped into Mohammed Ali Taj, a young friend of my father's. He was a poet, and I knew him from my Bhopal days when I ate on credit at his restaurant, the Ahad Hotel. Taj had come to Bombay because the producer S.M. Sagar, who made B-grade stunt movies, asked him to write lyrics for his film. Taj knew I was living on the studio premises, so he was good enough to introduce me to S.M. Sagar who gave me a job as his assistant at a hundred rupees a month.

Not only did my salary double, but Sagar Sahib also let me live in his house for free. Mrs Sagar was a most lovely and generous lady. They had four children, and I became very friendly with their three-year-old daughter, whom we called 'Baby'. This little girl did not sleep till I would tell her to go to bed. I was very attached to her. Many years later she came to say hello. Now, she's a grandmother.

I assisted Sagar Sahib on *Sarhadi Lutera*. For some reason the original dialogue writer had walked out of the project, and so Sagar Sahib asked me to write a few scenes for the film. I wasn't paid anything extra for writing, but I didn't mind that because, after all, I was living in his home for free.

It was during the making of *Sarhadi Lutera* that I met Salim Khan. He was playing Murad, the romantic lead in the film, and Sheikh Mukhtar was the 'sarhadi lutera'. Salim Sahib came across as a confident person and we became friends almost immediately. Soon, things started going wrong between Sagar Sahib and me because he had made some changes in the climax dialogue that I wrote, so I walked out. Anyone changing anything in my writing was unacceptable to me even then. It is said that beggars can't be choosers, but this beggar walked out. [*both laugh*]

I had no place to go, so I was back to sleeping in the Kamal Studio compound. Before this falling out happened, Sagar Sahib had introduced me to Brij Sadanah, who was making *Yakeen* for Deven Verma, and Brij hired me as an assistant in his unit. My salary was increased to 175 rupees per month. I wrote a few scenes for his film besides assisting him.

NMK: Were you an efficient assistant?

JA: Yes, I was. Despite that, within a few months, Brij Sadanah became quite unhappy with me.

NMK: Why's that?

JA. Somehow, he felt I regarded his work as incompetent. Though I didn't dare say it, my facial expressions must have been transparent. I was not surprised Brij was uncomfortable with me around. He was unsure what I thought of him, and I think his suspicions were right. [*both laugh*] Obviously, it was only a matter of time before I was thrown out from his unit. Back to square one.

Around that time, I met Hakeem Patanwala who was a bright, enterprising boy from a well-to-do Poona family. I have no idea why he had come to Bombay, but he landed here without a rupee to his name. He was so hard-working that it wasn't long before he was making good money by starting a business of his own hiring out high wattage bulbs for film shoots.

NMK: What did you learn as an assistant?

JA: I learnt different things from different people. Mr Kamal Amrohi's scripts made me aware that a character should have depth and dignity. But I don't think he was a great film technician.

One could say Brij Sadanah's films did not have depth—I don't think he cared about that either—but he knew the camera. He knew editing. He knew how to use a trolley shot, and why and when to use a zoom lens. He knew a lot about photography and could tell his cameraman which lens he wanted for a scene—75mm, 50mm, 25mm or 18mm. He knew the impact different lenses can achieve. I was most impressed by his understanding of film craft. I also learnt how to divide a scene into shots from him. He became a bit careless later on in his career, though if you see his *Yeh Raat Phir Na Aayegi, Ustadon ke Ustad, Yakeen* or *Afsana*, you will notice a certain finesse. Maybe his stories lacked substance, but there was an elegance and smartness in his shot divisions.

I was thrown out of Brij's unit, but I became great friends with his younger brother Chander Sadanah, who was his chief assistant. I still call him Chander Sahib. Through Chander, I met another friend, Ramesh Gupta. He was assisting some other director. They were both living in Evergreen, a guest house in Khar. I saw them quite often and they'd offer me dinner or whatever. I would even sleep in their room when I needed to. We would lay out a mattress roll on the floor, and I'd sleep there. Chander Sahib and Ramesh-ji were very kind and a great help to me in those days. Whenever I needed money Chander Sahib loaned it to me. I can't call it a loan as I never paid him back. I phoned him a few days ago. Sometimes, I call up old friends and have a chat. It's nice to hear their voices. When I completed fifty years in the film industry, we had a small party at my place, and I invited Chander Sahib and Ramesh-ji. I learnt certain things about film technique from Brij Sadanah, though my real takeaway from that experience was the quality of friendship that Chander Sahib and Ramesh-ji showed me.

NMK: What was Bombay like in the 1960s?

JA: Life was so different from what it is today, the city was so different—the cars, the roads, the way people dressed, the bands playing in hotels. Many things were different.

At that time 'matka' was very popular. It's a numbers game. You put chits with numbers written on them into a matka [a clay pot], then a chit is picked out of the pot, and the number on it is the winning number of the day.

Ratan Khatri, who died in 2020 at the age of eighty-eight, was called the Matka King. Instead of using chits, Khatri decided to change the practice from a 'matka' to a pack of playing cards to find the winning number. In a public place and in the presence of many, he asked strangers to pick three cards from a deck. The grand total of these cards was the opening number of the day, and then in the evening he did the same thing in some other part of the city and once again asked the public to pull out three cards. The total number of these three cards were the closing number. If you played 'open to close', it meant a double figure and you'd win ninety times what you had bet. So, one rupee could win you ninety rupees. Many studio workers, spot boys and production assistants were matka addicts—just about everybody played. I didn't, save this one time. My winning was a pure fluke.

As I have said, I didn't have a fixed spot to sleep in Kamal Studios and spent some nights in a corner of the studio near a huge peepal tree. This tree was opposite studio floor number one and under the tree there was a pump where we used to bathe. On the right-hand corner was Guru Dutt's small preview theatre. His brother Atma Ram looked after it, as Guru Dutt had passed away by the time I was living there.

At the entrance of studio floor number one there were some long planks and two wooden crates. They became my property. I took the two wooden crates, put a plank across them, and slept on it at nights. I did not have a dhurrie, sheet or pillow. I positioned this plank-bed in such a way that the light coming from floor one fell on me so I could read at night.

One day, I noticed that wherever I happened to look I'd see the number 81. A car enters the studio—it has the number plate 281. I needed to catch a bus, it was number 81. Number 81 seemed to be everywhere. So, for the first time in my life, I bet two rupees on 81.

My bet paid off and I won 180 rupees! I immediately rushed to Grant Road, bought a dhurrie, two bed sheets, a pillow and a pillowcase. The next night I laid down my dhurrie, sheet and pillow across my plank-bed and was just about to go sleep when all the boys sleeping in the same compound who were unemployed and struggling like me came to congratulate me. They praised the beautiful dhurrie and bed sheet, and as I had some money left from those 180 rupees, we went and had a drink to celebrate. They all accompanied me back to the plank-bed and wished me good night.

I kept those two bed sheets for years, even when I was living on Bandstand, I still didn't have the heart to throw them out. They were tattered and torn. Then, one day, they got lost.

NMK: Did you ever gamble again?

JA: I played again the next day and did not win, so I stopped and have never gambled since. It only worked once. Number 81.

NMK: You really lived through tough times. I mean sleeping on a plank across wooden crates.

JA: Those days have not left me because I still have vivid memories of those times. I am so grateful to life for having given me so much. Imagine where I started.

If I am having a grand meal or eating some delicacy, I ask myself, do I deserve this? When I am sitting in my car and I look outside the window and see people walking on the street or I see families living on the pavement, I ask myself, am I smarter and more talented than each one of them? There has to be someone in this crowd who must be extremely talented in some field but just could not get the right opportunity. Sometimes, it is just a random chance that puts you in the right place at the right time.

NMK: Did you ever think of giving it all up?

JA: There were some desperate moments, but it never occurred to me to give up, or to commit suicide or anything like that.

I look at my past today and I'm amazed by the optimism I had and wonder why it never abandoned me. Even in the worst of times

I had no doubt that I would make it one day, and bad days were just a passing phase. What made me think that? I don't know. It was totally foolish because things could have gone so wrong, and things do go wrong for many, but I firmly believed it was only a matter of time before my star would shine. This foolish optimism saw me through those bad times.

NMK: If optimism helped you, why do you call it foolish?

JA: If I could see my situation objectively, I could've become depressed. So, I was not objective. I remember when I was eighteen, my last pair of decent trousers got badly torn and there was no way I could wear them. It was a real problem, and it upset me, though somewhere at the back of my mind, I was happy it had happened, because I thought this could be the highlight of a book I'd write when I became somebody. Here was an eighteen-year-old boy who had no clothes to wear yet found it all amusing. I stayed in my room with a bed sheet wrapped around me till a friend of mine lent me a pair of trousers.

NMK: It's interesting how you saw events in your life as stories to be recounted in a book one day.

JA: Yes. What can you do with a man who is crazy? How can you demoralise him?

NMK: I remember reading a story about you sleeping in a costume room at Kamal Studio where you found the Filmfare Awards statuettes belonging to Meena Kumari. Did that really happen?

JA: It's a true story. At one point I was told by Kamal Amrohi's staff that I could live in an unused room where they stored costumes and props from the production of *Pakeezah*. There were many cupboards and drawers full of things, including artificial jewellery, clothes for men and women, shoes for the extras, etc.

One evening I opened a drawer and found several pairs of sandals. And right in the middle of those sad-looking, worn-out sandals I found three Filmfare Awards statuettes. I took them out of the drawer to examine them closely and realised they belonged to Meena Kumari—they were awards for her earlier films. I dusted the statuettes and put them in a row near the big mirror that dominated the room. In those days Filmfare Awards were like the Oscars for us and besides the National Award, this was the only film award we knew about. Whenever I found myself alone in that room, I locked the door from the inside, stood in front of the mirror with the statuette in my hand, and posed as if I had been awarded this trophy. The audience clapped and cheered me on, and I'd wave to them in recognition of their admiration. That was the first time I held a Filmfare Awards statuette in my hands and just imagine, here I was holding a statuette won by the great Meena Kumari!

NMK: I wonder if the director Farah Khan, Honey Irani's niece and therefore related to you, ever heard or read this story. She has a very similar scene in *Om Shanti Om* in which Shah Rukh Khan is holding a film award and giving an acceptance speech. It's all imaginary in the character's mind.

JA: Well, I have written about this incident, but I have serious doubts concerning Farah's reading habits! It's quite difficult to believe she would have read about it. [*smiles*] So I think she could have very well thought up the idea on her own.

NMK: Did you live alone in that costume room?

JA: No, I shared it with two others. One was Kafeel Aazar who was older than me and was Amrohi Sahib's assistant. Kafeel was a poet, and the nazm he wrote is still famous. It was sung by Jagjit Singh: 'Baat niklegi toh phir door talak jaayegi.' Kafeel did not make much of a mark on Hindi films as a lyricist and later left Bombay. [*JA sings: Baat niklegi toh phir door talak jaayegi*]

And the other person was Akhtar Farooqui, who later became an executive producer in Subhash Ghai's film company. I remember Akhtar Sahib said a young man wanted to marry his daughter Rehana who was living in Pune. He was coming over to meet him. Because this was a very new situation for Akhtar Sahib, he was rather nervous and wanted me around. The young man arrived and was none other than Subhash Ghai. That was the first time I met him. We decided to take Subhash to a drinking joint and spent the whole evening getting drunk on country liquor. By the time the 'interview' was over, all barriers between future son-in-law and father-in-law had broken down! We came back to the studio room, and we fell fast asleep. [*laughs*]

NMK: From those months of uncertainty, fantasising about winning awards and yet not knowing where your next meal was coming from to now—is Javed Akhtar the same person?

JA: Yes and no. Even when we try to become different, to some extent we remain the same. When we try to remain the same person, to a great extent, we become different.

NMK: How does that difference get informed by past experiences? Do past difficulties raise their heads in your memory?

JA: I often think of one night when everyone around me was sleeping in the studio compound. It was around 10:30 or 11 p.m. It had been three days since I had eaten, and I was so hungry I could not sleep. It was too late at night for me to go and borrow money from someone and buy something to eat. I was at the end of my tether. I was so hungry that my stomach hurt. Today, when I am sitting at my dining table and there's a huge spread of food in front of me, I sometimes think if I could have had only one of these dishes that night.

During my college years in Bhopal, sometimes I went hungry for days. Or if I had a high fever and no money to see a doctor, I was forced to rely on my immunity to get me better. These are some incidents that will always stay with me.

There was another time when I was about fourteen years old and travelling in a third-class compartment from Aligarh to Bombay—this was when I was going to Bombay to visit my father. There were a few senior students who were on the same train with me. The compartment was full and baking hot, there was not even a place to stand, and I was dying to sleep. I was so exhausted that I climbed up onto the upper berth and crawled into that steel net where luggage is usually kept. I was a thin boy so I could squeeze in. A little while later, I was woken up by the passenger on the berth below because my sweat was falling on him. I cannot tell you how traumatic that journey was. When I am lying on a luxurious bed in a five-star hotel, I think back to that train journey.

NMK: Despite these harrowing experiences, you don't sound like a victim.

JA: Remember, I was not living in permanent penury. My life was a roller-coaster ride. One day, I was at rock bottom and the next I was dancing the Foxtrot in a grand ballroom. [*smiles*]

Did I tell you about the time when I had to walk from Dadar to Bandra with only 20 naya paisa in my pocket?

You see, I had somehow developed a reputation that I could write comedy well. I was ghostwriting really, but I didn't mind. Once I was asked to write ten scenes for I.S. Johar, who was playing an estate agent in a film, which starred Joy Mukherjee and Vyjayanthimala. I forget the title of the film. The director-writer said that he could not write comedy and asked his assistant, who happened to be the dear friend of mine who I have already mentioned, Ramesh Gupta, to suggest someone. Ramesh took me to the producer, and it was agreed that I'd write ten scenes—100 rupees per scene, so 1,000 rupees. I wrote the ten scenes. When it came to paying me, the producer asked me to come to their office in Dadar and collect the money. I took a bus from Bandra, where I lived, and got down in Dadar. The office was somewhere near Ranjit Studio and when I got there, I found the door was padlocked.

There I was with only 20 naya paisa in my pocket. Now, how could I get home? I had two choices: I could take the bus back home—a 20 naya paisa ticket from Dadar would take me to the main road in Bandra and from there I could walk. Or I could buy something to eat and walk all the way to Bandra. It was almost 2 p.m. and I decided I had to eat something, so I bought 20 naya paisa worth of chanas [chickpeas], put them in my pocket, and started walking.

I crossed the Dadar bridge and passed Plaza cinema and took a right turn towards Bandra. As I was walking past the gates of Kohinoor Mill, I thought to myself, one day I'll drive by in my car and remember the day when my pocket was full of chana and I had no money for bus fare.

Years later, when Zoya was about eighteen, we were going somewhere in my car, and we happened to drive past Kohinoor Mill. I told Zoya about the whole sorry incident and how hungry I was on that day. She looked at me and then held my hand and said: 'In those days you must have got a lot of chickpeas for 20 naya paisa.'

For a second I was taken aback at her response. Then we both laughed. I love her for not giving me any sympathy.

NMK: Sounds like she has inherited your sense of humour! Did you often have no money for train or bus fare?

JA: I travelled without a ticket many times. I never had any money, though there were some days I wasn't confident enough to jump onto a train without being able to pay the fare.

One day, when I had not eaten anything and was very hungry, I decided to go and see Baldev, a friend of mine from Bhopal. He was the one we used to call 'Kaaley' when we were very young. He was a Sikh and was working in his brother's motor parts shop on

Grant Road. I thought Baldev would treat me to a meal and when I got to his brother's shop, I was told he had gone out. I didn't have the energy to walk all the way home, so I got onto the local train without a ticket and got down at the Khar station. A ticket-checker suddenly stopped me and asked to see my ticket. I said I didn't have one. He told me to stand aside and let the other passengers pass and when he finally turned to me, he said:

A ticket from Churchgate plus your fine is a total of thirteen rupees.

I was too exhausted to protest and replied: 'If I had thirteen rupees, I would not have travelled without a ticket. I don't have any money.' Then, looking at me, he said:

Then I'll have to put you behind bars.

I was beyond caring, thanks to hunger and frustration, so I told him he could do whatever he liked. The ticket-checker then asked me if I had a college education. I told him I was a graduate. He patted me on the back and said: 'Go, good luck.'

When I was doing well, I went a few times to Khar station to look for him. I described him to the staff at the ticket counter and explained that he was a short, fair-complexioned man with wavy hair. They couldn't figure out who he was. I never found him again. I'm still grateful to him and will not forget his pat on my back.

NMK: You clearly didn't have much money, so how did you spend your evenings?

JA: The early 1960s was a time when alcohol prohibition was still in force and so there were many illicit drinking joints in the city. Some were so huge that at any one time there could be 200 people drinking, smoking, and talking in what the Americans call a 'speakeasy'. The small shops around these drinking joints benefitted too as they sold sodas and kebabs and various snacks. There were some smaller drinking joints too, these were in private homes. These were often tiny two-room flats—regular lower-middle-class homes managed by the lady of the house, many of whom were Christian and were affectionately called 'aunty'. So 'aunty ka adda' had a regular clientele that sat at her two tables. She had a few chairs, and sometimes one could see a young boy doing his homework in the corner of the room or watch aunty cooking dinner in a nearby kitchen. One peg cost about 50 naya paisa—yes, it was as cheap as that! Aunty must've made around fifteen or twenty-five rupees a day. Some aunty ka addas came recommended to us as super exclusive and not just anyone was allowed in to drink the tharra, the country liquor that she made.

I went to many 'aunty ka addas' in the 1960s, though most often I could be found at 'Bailey ka adda'. Bailey Seth must have been in his mid-forties. He wore kurta-pyjamas and was a thin, short, fair-complexioned man. He had a two-bedroom flat on the ground floor of a Bandra building. His main room became the drinking area, and he lived in the other room with his wife, whom we never saw.

Bailey Seth was a fascinating character. His small joint had four tables and eight chairs. Two young boys who worked for Bailey Seth served his loyal clientele, which included Subhash Ghai, Shatrughan Sinha, the cameramen K.K. Mahajan and Sudarshan Nag, and even Mani Kaul.

One major advantage for us was that Bailey Seth gave us udhaar [credit], a facility not easily available anywhere in the world. He carefully noted down how much we owed him, and we paid him as and when we had some money.

Bailey Seth was very fond of drinking and dreamt that one day, he'd produce a film and compose the music for it. He could play the harmonium and saw himself as a great composer. When we had no money and wanted to drink some more, we'd egg him on:

Bailey Seth, bahut dinon se koi nayi tune nahin sunaayi aap ne. [You haven't played us one of your compositions for ages, Bailey Seth.]

Dekho yaar, yeh dhande ki vajah se bheja hi kharaab ho gaya, kuchh mind mein hi nahin aata. [This liquor business drives me crazy. I just can't think of a tune.]

He paused for a brief minute and then shouted out to one of his servants to bring him the harmonium. He performed certain rituals, touching his forehead to the instrument, etc., and after taking the cover off the harmonium, he started playing a tune. Those of us who had no money to pay for the next peg exclaimed loudly:

Wah, wah, bravo! What a tune, Bailey Seth! Unbelievable! This tune will catch on like fire.

He reassured us that he had many such catchy tunes ready for release and since we were all happily appreciating his music, it was time he offered us another peg! That's when he got emotional and said:

Did you know Dharmendra used to drink here? Even Raaj Kumar. But when film people become rich and famous, they forget everyone. And the same will happen to you all. You will forget me when you've made it.

Bailey Seth knew I was a struggling writer, so one evening he asked me:

Tu meri picture ka dialogue likhega? [Will you write dialogue for my movie?]

Bailey Seth, if you asked anyone else, I'll be mortally hurt.

He made me sign a promise note on a Bailey Productions' letterhead that I would write his dialogue one day. He looked at my signature and, calling out to his servant, said: 'Keep this paper safe. Get Javed another drink.'

One day, I went to his place earlier than usual; night had not yet fallen, and I had nothing else to do, so there I was. I saw Bailey Seth sitting alone. He was looking sad and depressed. I asked him what had happened.

Arey kya bataaun, time pe hafta deta hoon, phir bhi mereko raid kar diya, yaar. Javed, tereko ek baat bataun? Imaandaari ka zamaana hi nahin hai. [What can I say? I pay protection money on time, and I was still raided. Javed, shall I tell you something? The days of honesty have long passed.]

Here was this man who was never late in paying protection money to the police and yet he was raided. He was deeply hurt and felt that they had let him down. [*smiles*]

NMK: He didn't see the irony that he was running an illicit business!

JA: Clearly, he didn't.

NMK: Did your drinking partners and you remain friends in later years?

JA: Yes, of course. We all got to know each other well.

NMK: I imagine Mani Kaul was from a world different from yours.

JA: That's true.

I still remember arguing with him. Mani said a poet like Ghalib could only exist in India, and he was so right. At that time, I disagreed and said: 'Ghalib was a genius and wherever he would have been born, he would've written great poetry.' I was wrong and Mani was right. Ghalib's sensibility is in fact an excellent synthesis of Central Asia, particularly Persian culture and intellect, and Indian culture, tradition and philosophy. In a couplet, Ghalib says:

Na tha kuchh toh khuda tha, kuchh na hota toh khuda hota
Duboya mujh ko hone ne, na hota main toh kya hota
[When nothing existed, God existed. Were there nothing, God would exist. My very existence destroyed me. If I had not existed, what would have been.]

This is Vedantic philosophy. In Semitic religions, the Creator and the Creation are two identities but in Advaita they are not.

Everything is a manifestation of God and God is within everyone. And that is what Ghalib is saying in this couplet—if I did not exist, I would've been a part of God. My undoing is in my being. There is another couplet in which he speaks of cremation:

> Jala hai jism jahaan dil bhi jal gayaa hoga
> Kuredte ho jo ab raakh justuju kya hai?
> [If the body was burned, so was the heart. What do you seek now by scouring through the ashes?]

People are not cremated in Persia or in the Middle East or in Central Asia—they are cremated in India. Much of his verse makes you feel this is an Indian thought or the thought of an Indian.

I am so sorry that Mani Kaul is no longer with us. I would have liked to apologise to him.

NMK: Had you seen any of his films?

JA: No. But I remember when I was busy writing *Sholay*, *Deewaar* and *Don*, somebody asked me: 'Have you seen *Uski Roti* [His Bread]?' I said: 'No, I am busy seeing "apni roti [my bread]"!'

NMK: What happened to Bailey Seth?

JA: Life changed, and we had all gone our own ways. The late 1970s found me living in a bungalow at Bandstand—this was after *Sholay* and *Deewaar* and other films had been released. Sometime in 1978, my servant came to me one day and said:

> There's a man at the gate. He says his name is Bailey Seth and that you know him. He wants to meet you.

I was very happy and immediately said: 'Bulaao, jaldi [Call him in, hurry].' Bailey Seth came in and sat down. I could see he was not in a great shape. He was unshaven and wearing not very clean clothes. He told me he had left Bombay for a while—he had lost his flat and was now living somewhere in Sion, where he planned to start a liquor joint again. He needed money to furnish the place and buy the raw materials to make the alcohol. All I could do was to give him some money. Then I called Subhash Ghai who was another regular client of Bailey Seth's and told him he must help him too. I think Subhash gave him some money and that was the last time either of us saw him again. I don't know what happened to Bailey Seth after that.

NMK: What about your other drinking mates from the Bailey Seth days?

JA: I stayed in touch with Sudarshan Nag, the cameraman who also directed many films. He was an interesting man. I think he was from Himachal. He was a good cameraman and highly respected. So was K.K. Mahajan. KK was a loner, and a different kind of a person from Sudarshan who was more outgoing. I must make an honest confession here about a dialogue line in *Sholay*:

> *Aadhe idhar jaao, aadhe udhar jaao, baaqi mere peeche aao.* [Half of you go that way, the other half this way and the rest of you, follow me.]

While we were drinking one evening, Sudarshan said he thought some Hindi films were so illogical, and to prove how silly they were, he said they might even have dialogue like this. I thought his line was terrific. After many years, when writing *Sholay*, I decided to use it for Asrani's character. But this line really belongs to Sudarshan Nag.

NMK: Which other friend did you continue seeing from the Bailey Seth days?

JA: I told you about my friendship with Subhash Ghai. We met when he came to meet his future father-in-law—before the Bailey days. We spent many evenings together. I wrote the script for his *Meri Jung* and songs for *Kisna*.

I had another encounter with my past not so many years ago. Before I got a job at Kamal Studios, I often slept wherever I could lay my head down. One such place was under a big banyan tree which had a chabutara [a raised platform built around a tree for sitting] where many people came to sleep too. There was a small paan-beedi stall doing brisk business near the tree, and at the stall I met a gentleman, dressed in an undershirt and lungi, who used to come there to buy cigarettes. One evening, he told me he lived somewhere nearby in a small bungalow. He seemed like a nice man. I prefer not to name him.

We chatted from time to time and once or twice I even recited some poetry to him. He was quite fascinated by me, and he told me that he made stunt films. They were the C-grade kind—not even as grand as a Dara Singh film.

One day, he said:

Son, the rains will soon start, you'll have a problem sleeping outside, so you can sleep on my porch. It's not a problem for me. I will let my servants know.

I thanked him wholeheartedly and when the rains came, I started sleeping on his porch. I must have slept there for about a month. In the meantime, a friend of mine offered me a place to stay, so I did not see this kind gentleman again.

Many years passed. One evening, Shabana and I were visiting a friend and I had to send my driver on an errand, but then I remembered we had invited some people at her home in Janki Kutir in Juhu, so we decided to take a taxi and get back before the guests arrived. There were no mobiles back then, so I couldn't call our driver to come back and pick us up. When the taxi arrived, we sat in it and asked the driver to take us to Juhu. It was night-time. Suddenly, the driver said:

Javed, tumne mujhe pehchaana nahin? [Javed, you didn't recognise me?]

I looked at the driver's face in his rear mirror. He had a beard and looked old. I apologised, saying the light was poor and I was sorry, but I hadn't recognised him. He told me his name and then I realised he was the same producer who had let me sleep on his porch. He said:

Badi khushi hoti hai, bhai, jab akhbaar mein, magazine mein tumhaare baare mein padhta hoon, achcha lagta hai. Humein toh pehle se ummeed thi tumse. [I feel happy when I read about you in the papers and in magazines. You're doing well. I always expected great things of you.]

It all came back to me, and I remembered his kindness towards me. Then I panicked—how will I pay him for the ride? How can I offer him money? Obviously, I didn't have the guts to ask him what had happened and why he was driving a taxi. Had he lost his house? Where was he living? I felt so awkward.

When we got down, I asked: 'What does the meter say?' I phrased it as though the taxi meter was another person whom we both had to consult and it had nothing to do with us. He knew what I was doing and said:

Nahin, beta, bhool jao. Phir kabhi milenge. Paisa nahin loonga tumse. [No, son, never mind. We'll meet again. I can't take money from you.]

Saying that, he drove away. That was the last time I saw him.

I've had many such meetings and partings. Some encounters were very important to me, and you'd be surprised to know I had some encounters which did not even involve me meeting those people face-to-face.

The first took place when I was in Kamal Studios. They called me an assistant director—in fact, I was an errand boy, 'Bring me this, bring me that.'

After we wrapped for the day at Kamal Studio, I did not have much to do. I did not have any money to go out and enjoy a cup of tea in a restaurant. I couldn't even pay for that. So, after the studio office closed and all the admin staff had gone home, I'd sit in the office and dial up random phone numbers and chatted to anyone who picked up the phone. In those days, we had assistance numbers—193, 198, 173. They were information services that provided us with all sorts of information, including train schedules, or checking the time clock, etc.

I would dial one of these service numbers and talk to the operator, who was invariably a girl. We joked around and had innocent fun. I never crossed the line and never made any vulgar or indecent remarks. The phone operators enjoyed chatting because their job was not the most exciting job—they had to be on duty for hours on end, repeating the same information again and again.

One day, I came across a telephone operator who was witty and very intelligent. We became instant friends and ended up talking for forty minutes or more. We decided we had to find a way of connecting to each other again. Since the information services were answered by many operators working in shifts, how were we to find each other? We decided to have a code—I would ring up one of the service numbers and say the secret code. If the voice on the other line completed the code, that meant it was her, and we could start chatting again.

Our system worked and we managed to talk to each other regularly. Gradually, our relationship evolved into a serious one. I gave her my name and told her about my background and my problems. She gave me her name and spoke about her family—why she did not get along with her brother and his wife, though they all lived in the same house. We became really close friends. She gave me sound advice and kept encouraging me not to get depressed or bitter. She would say: 'If you want to be a writer or a director, you must never lose focus on your work.'

Time passed, and one night the executive producer at Mahal Pictures, S.K. Ojha, happened to call the office as he needed to talk to a staff member. He tried several times to get through and found the line constantly busy. That is how they found out that I was using the phone after office hours; something that was not allowed.

In a very gentle manner, S.K. Ojha explained things to me. He was a very kind person, someone else might have thrown me out. Instead, he advised me not to use the phone too often and added that having some innocent fun was natural at my age.

I made the fatal mistake of telling my phone friend that I had been discovered. She immediately said: 'You have only one job. You have a roof over your head, and if they throw you out, you won't even have a place to sleep. I cannot continue this relationship, it's too dangerous. I will never talk to you again.' She hung up and that was that. I tried desperately to find her; I called every service number for days on end, but she was gone from my life.

I don't know whether she is still alive or not. If she is, and if she reads this book, she is most welcome to call me, though she will have to use our code, so I know it's really her.

NMK: You remember the code?

JA: Of course, I do. I've never told anyone what it is.

NMK: Was it a number?

JA: No clues, Munni!

NMK: You said there was someone else that you became close to, and like your phone friend, you never met.

JA: This happened in the 1970s, a decade later. One day, I was sitting in my Bandstand house, Salim Sahib was there too, when the phone rang. He picked it up and heard a girl's voice. He kept talking to her as he was trying to guess who she was. She did not tell him her name. She talked to him for a while, and he later said to me that she sounded witty. We promptly forgot all about it.

A few days later, the girl called again and this time I picked up the phone and we talked. Then every so often she called and talked about poetry, film songs, novels and literature. She sounded young and bright. Not long after that her calls stopped, and a lady called and said: 'Mr Javed Akhtar? I'm calling to tell you that Ratri has died. I am her nanny.' I asked: 'Ratri? Ratri, who?' She said:

> Ratri used to call you. She was suffering from cancer and had a list of people whom she called when she was in acute pain. It distracted her. You were on her list. Ratri left me a note to say that when she passed away, I must inform everyone and thank them.

Her nanny told me that Ratri wrote poetry and that she was about eighteen years old. Sadly, I never got to meet her.

NMK: It's amazing how many people you've met at one point in your life, and how they managed to find you again later in life. A kind of full circle.

JA: Curious full circles. I'm sorry to use this word for want of a more modest one, but I think this must often happen to 'celebrities'. If you are not a known personality, you can get lost in the multitude, but when you become famous, other people can find a way to reach you. It has often happened to me—people whom I thought I had lost have got in touch again.

NMK: I never thought about it like that—that is indeed an advantage of being a celebrity.

JA: There were other people who I met again years later. I knew a girl called Charumati Deshpande, a debater from Government MLB College in Bhopal. She was an excellent speaker and a good singer. She and I competed in debates. If she came to know I was in the debating team, she sometimes refused to participate because she knew I would win. We had a kind of rivalry and friendship.

After many years, she contacted me. She was happily married and living in Hyderabad. She has a son who is grown up now. When I went to Hyderabad, she and her husband came to meet me. We talked excitedly about our college days.

I must not forget another such encounter. There was another girl who was a great debater. Her surname was Masoor. I don't remember her first name, so I hope she'll forgive me if I refer to her by her last name. She once argued superbly in a Rotary Club debate, but I was given the trophy. It was probably because I had won two years in a row and people may have assumed I merited the trophy again. Though they all congratulated me, I was not happy. I told Masoor that she deserved to win and not me. I felt even more uncomfortable because some boys from my college took me out in an open car, shouting about my victory. It was embarrassing. In my heart of hearts, I knew she deserved the trophy. In later years, when I visited Bhopal, I asked college friends if they knew what had happened to Masoor. Somebody told me she had been bitten by a snake and was dead. I was upset to hear that.

Many years passed and one day a girls' school in Bhopal invited me to address their pupils. I sat in the principal's office, and she offered me coffee and biscuits. Then she said:

> You obviously don't remember me, but I have met you before. I was competing in the Rotary Club debate opposite you.

The principal was none other than Masoor. After we had tea, we talked a little about the past. I was so pleased to meet her again. She then took me to the large hall where I was to address the girls in the school. I started off by telling them about the debate and that the trophy that I had won really belonged to their principal and not to me.

NMK: You said you got the trophy because of your reputation. Was it also because men were assumed to be better at everything than women? How did your upbringing influence the way you saw the position of women in society?

JA: I don't think it was a gender issue. I was about seventeen and she must've been about the same age.

Regarding the second part of your question, my aunt and mother were working women. They were college and university lecturers. And my Naani was a domineering woman who dominated her husband. I have lived all my life with women who were decision-makers. I never saw any male family member talking rudely to a woman, whether it was my father or my uncle. They were so respectful and polite while talking about their wives. They would say:

Hamida keh rahin thein, not Hamida yeh boli.
[using the polite form of 'she was saying']

You may think I am naïve, but till the age of twenty, I knew nothing about domestic violence. I had not witnessed it or heard about it. I did not know anybody who had raised a hand against a woman. Relatives and neighbours, the academic staff, whether in Lucknow or Aligarh, were made up of men who were respectful to women. Not just in my family, everyone in my social circle treated women with respect as well. There was no swearing or physical violence. I think the first sign of a mean person is if he doesn't respect the woman in his life.

NMK: May I go back to the mid-1960s. How soon after you arrived in Bombay in 1964 did you form a writing partnership with Salim Khan?

JA: Two years later. And in those two years, between 1964 and 1966, I somehow managed to earn something by working as an assistant or doing some ghostwriting for films. I had no fixed address and moved from place to place. At one point, I ended up sharing a room with my friend Hakeem Patanwala, whom I've mentioned before. We shared the monthly 120 rupees rent for a room in a bungalow called Lilos. Lilos was near St. Anne's Church in Bandra and was a decent enough place, so that became one of my many homes.

One day, Hakeem decided to go back home. Now, how was I to find his share of the rent? A friend asked me if he could move in, but I didn't believe he could pay sixty rupees every month. I said no to him and told him: 'Where will you find sixty rupees each month? Because of you, I'll get thrown out of the house.' That friend was Shatrughan Sinha! [*laughs*] Finally, it was another friend called Bindu, Manmohan Desai's chief assistant, who ended up sharing the room with me.

As Lilos happened to be close to Salim Sahib's place in Bandra, we started spending many evenings together. Salim Sahib was married, and his son Salman was about seven months old at the time. We talked about stories and screenplays. He had narrated a story to Brij Sadanah, who decided to make it into a film with Ashok Kumar, Jeetendra and Mala Sinha. It was called *Do Bhai*. The film did not run. The story had been distorted beyond recognition, otherwise it was a good story.

Whenever we met, Salim Sahib told me I had a talent for writing and if I could write good dialogue for a film like *Sarhadi Lutera*, imagine what I could do in a good film. I was disenchanted with dialogue writing after my experience on *Sarhardi Lutera* and *Yakeen*, but he encouraged me not to give it up. One day, we were sitting at his place when S.M. Sagar Sahib dropped in. He showed us a short story he had found in the Hindi magazine *Madhuri*. It had a good plot twist, though the narrative was not long enough for a two-and-a-half-hour film. So, he asked us to write a screenplay based on the story and offered 2,500 rupees each. It was a little fortune for us, so naturally we agreed. We wrote the screenplay in eighteen days and gave it to Sagar Sahib. He paid us in full but did not give us a screen credit. There was nothing we could say. The film was *Adhikar*. It was released in 1971.

NMK: You may be interested to know that the Wikipedia page does credit Salim–Javed for the screenplay, but IMDb does not.

JA: Oh really? Working on that film helped us because it so happened that Sudhir Wahi, Sagar Sahib's assistant, was aware that we had written the screenplay of *Adhikar* and suggested we get in touch with

Narendra Bedi, who was directing a film for Sippy Films. Sudhir said Sippy Films wanted to create a story department and were looking for writers. I remember Salim Sahib telling me: 'They're too big a company, they won't employ us.'

All this was happening in December 1969. Sudhir Wahi said he had fixed us an appointment on the following Monday with Narendra Bedi and Ramesh Sippy. We did not go on the Monday, or on Tuesday. I found myself alone on Wednesday and, after I had my lunch in an Irani hotel, I thought: 'I'm free. I don't have any other work. Let me go and meet them.' I still had a bit of money left over from the 2,500 rupees that Sagar Sahib paid me, so I took a taxi to the office of Sippy Films on 14th Road in Khar.

At the meeting, I explained to Narendra Bedi and Ramesh Sippy that Salim Sahib and I write as a team. Ramesh Sippy was twenty-six and I was twenty-five. Bedi said there was a film that was about to be released called *Kati Patang* and it had a very good screenplay. I said I had not seen the film, but if we cannot write better than that film's screenplay, then we can't claim to know how to write. They were somewhat taken aback by my confidence.

I was asked to bring Salim Sahib along to our next appointment. As we were making our way to their office in Khar, I asked Salim Sahib:

How much should we ask for?

A thousand rupees a month.

A thousand rupees! What are you saying? They'll throw us out!

Till then, I had not even made 250 rupees per month, but Salim Sahib was confident they'd pay us 1,000 rupees. He had guts in such matters and reassured me: 'There's no harm in asking, is there?'

When we settled down for our meeting at Sippy Films, I narrated a story to them. Immediately after the narration, I remember Ramesh Sippy saying: 'Your claim about your writing seems to be right!' Clearly, the story of a doctor I had narrated impressed them. Then Narendra Bedi took us into another room and asked what salary we wanted. 'A thousand rupees.' He said: 'We'll give you 750 rupees each per month for a three-month trial period. After that, if all goes well, we'll pay you 1,000 rupees.' [*smiles*]

The next day, when we went to Sippy Films, we were told to work on the screenplay of *Andaz,* a film which was almost half shot. They did not have a satisfactory second half or a powerful climax. Salim Sahib promptly thought up a terrific climax and narrated it to them within fifteen minutes. [*both laugh*]

So that's how we came to work at Sippy Films. We were there for almost seven years and our salary remained 750 rupees! It was a token amount because they paid us separately for dialogue writing and screenplays. For *Seeta aur Geeta,* we were paid 15,000 rupees, 25,000 rupees for *Sholay,* and by the time *Shaan* was made our price had risen. Though the 750 rupees a month remained the same and was always paid to us.

We took about a month to complete the screenplay of *Sholay* for Ramesh Sippy, and it took about twenty days for Yash Chopra's *Deewaar.* When the screenplay of *Deewaar* was ready, I needed a further twenty to twenty-two days to write the dialogue. These scripts were the only versions. There was not a second, third or tenth draft! There was no rewriting.

When I was writing the *Deewaar* scene where the two brothers meet under the bridge, the first line that came to my mind was the last dialogue: 'Mere paas Maa hai.' Then I started writing the scene from the beginning to reach this last line.

NMK: That's fantastic! It is one of the most famous lines of Indian cinema!

I am a bit confused about *Haathi Mere Saathi.* How did that screenplay fit into the Sippy period?

JA: We met Rajesh Khanna often because he came to Ramesh Sippy's office in the evenings, and we all drank together. Sippy Films had given Rajesh Khanna an early break. By 1969, he had two superhits in *Aradhana* and *Do Raaste* and Rajesh Khanna became a superstar overnight. One day, he said:

> I've signed a picture with a South Indian producer who has given me a huge amount. Two lakhs fifty thousand rupees. With that money I am paying an advance on a bungalow on Carter Road that belongs to Rajendra Kumar and I have promised to pay the balance within six months. You must rewrite the script. The story has four elephants and a hero—that cannot change, though everything else can.

Rajesh Khanna then added with a smile:

> The script is so terrible, but if returned the money, I would lose the house. And if I did the film, I would lose my acting career!

Rajesh was in a bind, so we decided to work on the script which was based on a Tamil film *Deiva Cheyal*. We didn't like the screenplay, so we made major changes while Inder Raj Anand wrote the dialogue. In 1971, the script we wrote became *Haathi Mere Saathi* and that was remade in Tamil in 1972 and called *Nalla Neram*.

So, you have a remake from Tamil to Hindi finding itself remade back from Hindi to Tamil. You can imagine how different our screenplay was from the original. That is how Salim Sahib and I came to write *Haathi Mere Saathi*. We got 10,000 rupees for it and Rajesh Khanna got his bungalow!

NMK: This is an aside—but who borrowed this phrase 'angry young man' in India. This was a title given to a group of British playwrights and novelists that included John Osborne and Kingsley Amis. Osborne's *Look Back in Anger* helped to create the concept of 'angry young men', men who were angry with the status quo and who identified with the working class.

JA: Salim Sahib and I did not use this label to describe Amitabh Bachchan's character; it was the press who did. I think it just caught the imagination of the media.

NMK: I see. Where were you living in the early 1970s when *Seeta aur Geeta* and *Zanjeer* were released? I am sure your circumstances had changed by then, plus you had recently married.

JA: Honey and I were living in Juhu. Farah Khan's father, Mr Kamran Khan, kindly gave us a flat that we rented for three hundred rupees. As you know, Farah's mother, Menaka Irani, is Honey's eldest sister. So, Kamran Sahib was my brother-in-law. He owned three flats in a Juhu building. The flat we were living in could have been rented for much more, but it was his way of helping us keep our self-respect.

In the meantime, I saved up some money and took some money from Salim Sahib so we could buy our first home and in 1974, I managed to buy a lovely sea-facing flat in Bandstand Apartments in Bandra West. It was an exclusive building where most of the occupants were Parsis. At first, the tenants were sceptical about selling a flat to someone working in films, but ultimately they agreed. The flat cost us peanuts when we compare to house prices today. But, for me, even those peanuts were a fortune back then! But can you imagine two bedrooms, two bathrooms and a hall in a beautiful building costing under one lakh rupees? It's impossible today. You can't even buy a shed for that.

NMK: Salim Sahib lent you the money?

JA: Oh yes. That's how we both bought our first homes. He got a flat in Galaxy Apartments further down on Bandstand, which was double the price of my place. He still lives there with his family. I gave him whatever money I had, and we had to borrow some money to top it up.

NMK: Did you borrow the money from the bank?

JA: No! It was not possible to borrow money to buy property in those days. I'm talking about the 1970s. Some friends lent us the money. We didn't have much money when Honey and I got married.

I remember a producer suggested we should host a grand reception to celebrate our wedding, invite lots of people, and that way I'd get some money together because many give money to the young couple instead of a gift. I did not follow his advice, of course!

Within a couple of years, in 1976 or 1977, I could afford to buy a larger home, and we bought a double-storeyed bungalow, also on Bandstand, where Honey and Zoya now live. Thankfully, the lack of money stopped being a problem.

NMK: I'm curious to know if your family raised you to think money was not important

JA: No, no, money was important. I needed a roof over my head and two square meals. And I had a family too. I believe that despite the fact that money is very important, I think it's highly overrated. People want to make money for money's sake. I want to make money to buy comforts and luxuries.

NMK: Luxuries?

JA: Luxuries! Yes! Money is not the end, for me it is the means. One should not bother about it too much. One should not worry about spending—one should worry about earning! I have many fantasies. For example, I like the idea of buying a yacht and a private jet someday. I can't tell people about these fantasies because they'll think I'm crazy.

NMK: You surprise me!

I'd like to come back to the 1970s. Why did you decide on Salim–Javed as a screen name rather than Khan–Akhtar?

JA: It sounded better, whereas Khan–Akhtar didn't sound good. I was known as Javed; no one called me Akhtar. In the beginning, Salim Sahib hesitated because his screen name as an actor was Prince Salim. He said:

> There's a problem. People know me as Prince Salim, and they won't know who Salim is.

I assured him: 'It's a matter of a year or two. They will all know you. Don't worry!' Obviously, his name had to come before mine because he's almost ten years older than me.

NMK: You've often said you didn't want to talk about how you worked as a team. Can we talk about it here?

JA: We really didn't sit down and plan how we would divide the work. It just happened organically.

The basic stories came from Salim Sahib. *Seeta aur Geeta* was an idea based on *Ram aur Shyam*. Ramesh Sippy suggested it to us. He said we should take the *Ram aur Shyam* story and adapt it to a story about two girls, Seeta and Geeta. Prakash Mehra's *Haath ki Safai* was another film we adapted. Those rights were bought from the producer of *Do Ustad*, starring Raj Kapoor, Madhubala and Sheikh Mukhtar. I can't think of many films after that which were adaptations. The storylines nearly always came from Salim Sahib, whether it was *Sholay*, *Deewaar*, *Trishul* or *Don*, and together we developed them into screenplays, and I wrote the dialogue.

The basic twists, even the persona of the angry young man, who became so famous, were Salim Sahib's ideas.

NMK: Can you elaborate on the difference between a storyline and a screenplay?

JA: Salim Sahib would think of a story that could be narrated in ten minutes. We then developed it, scene by scene, into a screenplay for a two-and-a-half-hour film, obviously during the development of the screenplay many characters were introduced into the narrative.

I'll give you the example of *Sholay*: there's a Thakur who hires two young men to protect his village against a nasty villain who had chopped off Thakur's arms—all this came from Salim Sahib.

In the case of *Sholay*, Ramesh Sippy was also part of writing the screenplay, though he was not credited as such.

As far as *Sholay* was concerned, the original idea was centred on an army officer who loses his hands because a hand grenade explodes in them. He returns to his village and is told a dacoit is harassing his village. So, he hires two young recruits expelled from the army. That was the original story. Gradually, the army officer became a police officer, the expelled recruits became two handsome hoodlums. The heroines entered the screenplay and so did all the other characters.

NMK: A friend of mine said the plot of *Sholay* resembled *Mera Gaon Mera Desh*.

JA: Nobody compared *Mera Gaon Mera Desh* to *Sholay* at the time of the release. Some people said the influence of Sergio Leone was very strong. Yes, that was true. We loved his films, and he did influence us, but other films impacted us too. We've talked about how Indian film classics, including *Mother India, Gunga Jumna* and *Mughal-e-Azam* impacted us. As far as writing the dialogue was concerned, I was very influenced by the progressive writers of Urdu literature, such as Krishan Chander. Another influence was the crime writer Ibn-e Safi. We were also influenced by American paperbacks—pulp fiction—and Hollywood films. We read all the works of James Hadley Chase, Raymond Chandler and others. If I liked a novel, I'd give it to Salim Sahib to read and vice versa. I was a chain-reader! The moment I finished one novel, I'd start another on the very same day. I had read the great classics in my college days, but we learnt how to communicate from popular novels. As a dialogue writer, at least I did. I learnt the power of one-liners. Short statements. Those American novels taught me understatement and restraint. That was the beauty of our characters, they were restrained, yet you could sense a volcano bubbling inside them that could erupt at any time.

NMK: When *Sholay* was released, some critics in the West called it a 'Curry Western' and in India some thought the film was based on *Once Upon a Time in the West.*

JA: As I said, we were influenced by Sergio Leone. The critics also said *Zanjeer* was *Dirty Harry*. It must be remembered that *Dirty Harry* was released in December 1971 and *Zanjeer* in May 1973. It would've been impossible for us to have written the screenplay, had the film shot, and edited and released in such little time. It's all rubbish. The basic story of *Zanjeer* was Salim Sahib's brainchild. Later we wrote the screenplay together. *Dirty Harry* was remade in Hindi, though not by us. It was called *Khoon Khoon* and turned out to be a big flop.

What *Zanjeer* and *Dirty Harry* had in common were their heroes: two angry police officers. That's about it. Though I think *Zanjeer*'s hero has more layers.

Whenever some Indian film critics saw a film of ours, they assumed it had to be a copy and couldn't believe we could think up ideas ourselves. Think of the twist in *Don*. Vijay is planted in a gang by a police officer to expose the bad guys, then the police officer gets killed in the line of duty. Without the police officer to back up his story, Vijay has a hard time convincing the police that he's an undercover agent, while the gang has guessed he's a plant. So, we have a situation where both the police and the gang are after Vijay's blood. What a fantastic twist! All Salim Sahib.

NMK: What about that line 'Don ko pakadna mushkil hi nahi namumkin hai'? This is definitely you.

JA: I plead guilty as charged! [*smiles*]

NMK: Writing a screenplay together is like clapping with both hands. One cannot exist without the other.

JA: That's right. We were the two hands. Sometimes, people tend to undermine Salim Sahib in private conversations. I've heard it many times and I've always corrected them. This is something that must be made clear beyond any doubt that he was the major contributor in our partnership. To say it was all Javed is utter rubbish! The fact is that most storylines were his. The screenplays were written together, while I wrote the dialogue.

NMK: All the dialogue?

JA: Yes. That was my department.

NMK: What do you need to write good dialogue?

JA: You need a huge vocabulary to write different characters who belong to different social milieus and age groups. You must be obsessed with language. You should have an ear for dialects, unusual expressions and metaphors. And if you hear an interesting phrase, you must be able to recall it later without any effort.

The same approach applies to songwriting. I wrote a song for Shyam Benegal's *Sardari Begum*, which was a realistic film, and the vocabulary had to match the language spoken seventy to eighty years ago. A thumri had to sound like a traditional thumri. The same for a kajari or a ghazal.

When I wrote the songs for *Lagaan*, they had a rural fragrance, while the *Silsila* songs needed a sophisticated, educated touch and had to sound like the language of a poet. And the songs of *Rock On!!* had to sound like tracks on an album by a young band and not like film songs.

NMK: Writing an exchange between hero and villain in the same scene requires lines that get the psychologies of both hero and villain right. How do you make sure you're doing that?

JA: You must identify with the characters and understand their psyche. Your words are mirrors of their morality and aesthetics. How could anyone with a grain of compassion look at a man writhing in agony and say:

Kaisa phadphada raha hai.

By using this verb, Gabbar is dehumanising Thakur. For him, Thakur is a creature, not a human being. The verb 'phadphadana' usually describes a bird.

NMK: You could translate 'phadphadana' as fluttering or flapping about. A cruel word to describe a human being's agony. Is finding an appropriate vocabulary for a character intuitive in your case?

JA: There's no other way. With experience writers choose words instinctively, we don't always have to overthink.

NMK: Many of your screenplays are considered lessons in film writing. Did you narrate the screenplay as per the usual practice in Indian cinema? Or did Salim–Javed give the directors a bound script to read?

JA: Although we gave the director and his team bound scripts, narration was the tradition. We did have to narrate our screenplays to the heads of department and the actors. Sometimes, we were obliged to give several narrations as someone from the unit may have been absent at the first reading. Narrating the screenplay usually took around two-and-a-half hours and in between we sat around talking with the film unit. I thoroughly enjoyed narrating scripts.

NMK: Did you and Salim Sahib suggest camera positions in your screenplays? For example, did you say such and such dialogue should be filmed in mid-shot or close-up?

JA: We wrote in minute detail and even listed the props. There should be a cupboard here and a table there. Some directors followed our suggestions and others didn't.

I don't see how you can write appropriate dialogue without visualising a scene in its entirety. There were people who said, somewhat exaggeratingly, that Salim–Javed write in such detail that anybody can take a camera and shoot the film. That wasn't quite true.

NMK: Were you good at narrating?

JA: I was known for my narrations. People said I was a great narrator and had everyone gripped.

I am not sure I'd like to name the producer, though he was someone for whom we had written many hit films. His connection with the universe, I'm afraid, was through his own voice. The minute he stopped talking, he switched off. It became an obsession for me to hold his attention beyond scene twelve. And I invariably failed. By scene twelve, he was fast asleep. It finally stopped bothering me and I continued the narration to the cast and crew regardless of his loud snoring. [*both laugh*]

NMK: What was the first narration you ever gave?

JA: Oh, that was tragic. Remember Parvez, the young publicist with whom I shared a room? Well, he was working for Mr Mahipatray Shah, the producer who made the 1965 film *Purnima* with Meena Kumari and Dharmendra. The film had some songs by Gulzar and the music was composed by Kalyanji–Anandji. Once the film had been completed, they were looking for another story, so Parvez recommended that I go and narrate a story to them. This was before Salim Sahib and I became writing partners.

At the appointed time I arrived at their office and was told that Mr Shah and his accountant would listen to the story. Within ten minutes of my starting, Mr Shah yawned. One minute later, his accountant yawned. I kept narrating, pretending I hadn't noticed. Shah Sahib yawned again and then the accountant yawned. Yawn followed yawn. Very soon there was a jugalbandi of yawns! I was only twenty-one years old and got so nervous that I started sweating and asked them if I should stop. They said: 'Why are you stopping? Go on.'

I continued narrating and they continued yawning. During the whole session, narration and yawning ran in parallel. When I finished, Mr Shah smiled and said: 'We'll let you know.' I never heard from him again. That was my first experience of narrating a film story. By the way, it was the same story that got us our job at Sippy Films. So, one producer's meat can be another producer's poison!

NMK: Were there other unusual narrations?

JA: I once narrated a story to Babubhai Bhanji, a stunt film producer, who listened with keen interest. At the end of the narration, he said: 'Darling ...' In those days every man in the film industry was 'Darling' and every woman was 'Madam'.

Darling, teri story toh achchi hai. Magar iss mein ek rishk hai ... [Darling, your story is good but it's risky ...]

Risk, sir? What risk?

Ye story aaj tak kisi picture mein aayi nahin hai. [This story hasn't been seen before in any picture.]

Those were his exact words. He didn't want anything original and here I was trying to present him with a new concept, a new screenplay, a new idea. All I could do was to leave his office, saying: 'You're right, sir. I am sorry. This story has not been made into a film before.'

NMK: How did you get to meet other producers?

JA: You won't believe it, but after the release of *Zanjeer,* and for almost nine months, we had not signed a single film because we decided to stick to our rates—two lakh rupees for a script. Don't forget two lakh rupees in those days was like asking for ten crore! But we stuck to our guns. We had a sense of security since we were still being paid 750 rupees every month by Sippy Films. Meanwhile, I bought a second-hand Ambassador car for 13,000 rupees. I spent all the money I had on the car and had no money for petrol. Salim Sahib's wife, Salma Bhabhi, gave me fifty rupees so I could buy petrol. Ultimately, I had to sell the Ambassador.

It was around that time I was invited to a party to celebrate the completion of *Yaadon ki Baaraat*. Nasir Hussain Sahib was very fond of throwing big parties on the vast lawn of his house. At this party, an important producer met me—let's not use his name—and he said:

Javed, if you have any good story, narrate it to me because I need a good script.

Sir, we have a film script with dialogue, and everything is ready, but the price is the problem. No one is willing to pay the price we want.

No, no, money is not a problem. I want a good script and if your script is good, I'll take it. Come to my office and narrate it to me.

I told Salim Sahib about my encounter. We fixed a suitable time, and I went alone to see the producer. Before I started narrating, I said:

I won't ask for a rupee in advance, but I must tell you the price of the script now, just in case you like it. If I tell you the price later, you may think I'm hiking the fee because you liked the story.

OK, what's the price?

Two lakhs.

There was dead silence. He said nothing, I said nothing. Then he pressed a bell, a peon entered, and he told the peon to call his partner, who was in the other room. The producer didn't look at me and I had no idea what he was thinking. I thought maybe he wanted to discuss the price with his partner. His partner entered the room, looking hassled and preoccupied: 'Yes, what is it?' The producer turned to me and smilingly said:

Jo tu mereko bola, isko bhi bol. [Repeat what you just told me.]

Two lakhs for the script.

They burst out laughing—they thought it was the most ridiculous thing they had ever heard.

NMK: How funny! Talking about narrations, how amazing it would be if your narrations of *Deewaar* or *Sholay* had been filmed! They'd be serious archive material today. Did anyone in the team take notes while you were narrating?

JA: No one did. But Amitabh Bachchan had an unusual habit. Before shooting an important scene, he would call me to his make-up room and ask me to narrate the scene to him again. I think he wanted to be reminded of the tone of dialogue delivery. Amitabh is a good listener. Even when you're talking to him casually, you can sense he listens attentively. This is a rare quality. Quite often, we give the impression of listening when in fact we are waiting to talk.

NMK: Where did you first meet him?

JA: We were shooting the last few scenes of *Seeta aur Geeta* and on an adjoining set, *Anand* was being shot. So, we went to say hello to Rajesh Khanna on his set. Amitabh was there too. He did not have any dialogue in that shot; all he had to do was stand behind Rajesh and watch him sing the song, 'Kahin door jab din dhal jaaye'. Salim Sahib had met Amitabh at Mr N.C. Sippy's before I did, and it was he who introduced me to Amitabh Bachchan.

I was standing outside the studio floor and when Amitabh's work for the day was done, I saw him waiting for his taxi. He was wearing wide camel-coloured bell bottoms and an off-white shirt. He seemed a cultured and polite young man to me. We exchanged a few pleasantries—someday we must work together, blah, blah, blah. Nothing of much significance. The taxi came and he left.

It was his presence on the screen that really impressed me. In *Parwana*, he played a dark character called Kumar and the scene in which he comes to Ashok Verma [Om Prakash] and desperately tries to convince him to give his niece's hand to him really surprised me. Verma refuses and then the furious Kumar kills him. I can never forget his presence. You could see he was a volcano, bursting with fiery anger. Had anyone seen such a powerful performance before? In a montage in *Guddi*, Hrishikesh Mukherjee used a shot from the same scene.

Bombay to Goa was the next film that had a striking performance by Amitabh. In one scene he is sitting munching a sandwich and Shatrughan hits him, he falls off his chair and when he gets up, he is still munching that sandwich. I was floored by his intensity and his cool. And I think I am the only person, along with the film's producer, who has seen his super flop *Raaste kaa Patthar* three times. It was playing at Gaiety Galaxy and for the first three days after its release, I went to see it for Amitabh. That same man was dancing and looking happy while the heroine was singing a song on Juhu beach. His anger and intensity disappeared when he was doing comedy. What people did not realise at the time was that his films had awful screenplays and bad stories—despite that he did impeccable work. If the same films had become hits, everything about them would have been considered good. When a film bombs, everything about it is regarded as bad. I think that's silly because a good performance can be part of a bad film. I was convinced that he was one of the greatest actors on the Hindi screen. There was not an iota of doubt in my mind.

And then *Zanjeer* came. *Zanjeer* was originally written for Dharmendra, and for some reason Dharam-ji refused the film because there was discord between some of his relatives and Prakash Mehra. Family counts more than anything for Dharam-ji. So *Zanjeer* had no lead actor, and Prakash Mehra was starting his production, so he went from star to star. Everybody refused.

NMK: Dev Anand too?

JA: Yes, Dev Sahib too. We narrated the *Zanjeer* script to many stars, dialogue by dialogue. In retrospect, I think their refusal was understandable. Remember this was Rajesh Khanna's peak period, Laxmikant–Pyarelal and R.D. Burman were dominating the charts.

Music and romance was the currency of the day. And here you have a script where the hero is not singing, not romancing, not even smiling. There were other screen heroes who were angry like Birju in *Mother India* or Gunga in *Gunga Jumna*, but they had time for romance and comedy while showing all the characteristics of a real hero. Whereas our man, Vijay, was undiluted anger and bitterness, no romance, no comedy, no songs, nothing. Obviously, it was a shock to every actor. No one was willing to accept the *Zanjeer* role. Prakash Mehra had even asked Navin Nischol—that didn't work out either. Most actors would say:

Bhai, yeh kis type ka hero hai? [What kind of hero is this?]

In the meantime, I kept trying to persuade Prakash Mehra to cast Amitabh. Before I managed to convince him, I called Amitabh and told him:

We have a script, and I'm trying to have you cast in the film. Can I come and see you?

He asked me over right away. He didn't have work in those days, and was often at home. I noted his address and went to his house—it was a very small bungalow called Mangal on 14th Road in Juhu. I narrated the entire script of *Zanjeer* to him. I did this without Prakash Mehra having a clue about it. I still remember Amitabh's reaction when I finished the narration. He looked at me with surprise in his eyes and said:

Do you think I can pull this role off?

I am quoting the exact words he used. I assured him that no one could play the role better. He was a bit confused about why I was so confident because till then Amitabh had been playing poets and doctors and so on.

At that stage Prakash Mehra had not met Mr Bachchan. So, I planned to introduce them to one another. I called Amitabh and found out where he was shooting. He said the next day he would be

at Rajkamal Studio in Parel for *Gehri Chaal*. I took Prakash Mehra
there and, in the make-up room, I introduced him to Amitabh and
his brother Ajitabh who was there too. Everything else followed.

One thing is true—I did not realise it at that time, though I do
now, and I want to salute Prakash Mehra—here was a successful
director who had taken a script from writers who were not that
famous, though we had written some successful films like *Haathi
Mere Saathi*, *Seeta aur Geeta* and *Andaz*, people knew who Salim–
Javed were, but that was about all. There was no great aura around
us. That happened only after *Zanjeer*, and yet Prakash Mehra wanted
our story; a story that was rejected by one star after another. He did
not give up.

NMK: Did he change anything in the script?

JA: Not at all. He said if he was going to make the film it would be
as the script dictated. Hats off to him.

Today, if you take a script to a producer and a star tells him that
it is not up to the mark, the producer will dump you and the script
without batting an eyelid. But Prakash Mehra accepted our script
and cast Amitabh Bachchan just on our say-so. I am not claiming the
entire credit, but I did keep persuading Prakash Mehra. That said, I
was not producing the film; I was not putting my money where my
mouth was, Prakash Mehra was. He had the guts to cast this young
man, who had some six or seven flops behind him, and who the
distribution community had decided would never succeed as an actor.

During the shooting of *Zanjeer*, Prakash Mehra realised he had
made the right choice. It dawned on him that he had struck gold.
He once told me: 'I have decided I will never make a film without
him.' Manmohan Desai felt the same way about Amitabh and always
chose to cast him after *Amar Akbar Anthony*. Manmohan Desai and
Prakash Mehra were Amitabh's two important directors.

With Amartya Sen.

With Dr Muhammed Yunus.

With President Barack Obama, Shabana Azmi and Salman Khurshid at a dinner hosted by the former prime minister, Manmohan Singh, who is seen in the background with Michelle Obama. 2010.

With Lata Mangeshkar.

With Asha Bhosle.

Winning the *Filmfare* Award. Seen here with Alka Yagnik and A.R. Rahman.

With Shankar Mahadevan and Shabana.

With Pandit Shivkumar Sharma and Nusrat Fateh Ali Khan.

With Farhan and Zoya at a screening of *Gully Boy*.

Celebrating Holi with Shabana and Zoya.

His brother Salman Akhtar is a celebrated psychotherapist who lives and works in America. He has written several books and writes poetry in both English and Urdu.

Javed Akhtar considered Farhan Mujib his closest friend and a renaissance man. They first met when they were both twelve years old. Their friendship endured through the years. Farhan Mujib is seen here with his wife Fouzia who is also a close family friend.

Seen in these photographs with his favourite singer, Kishore Kumar, and favourite composer, R.D. Burman, who have been collaborators in the creation of many memorable songs, including the popular 'Ek Ladki ko Dekha'.

With former prime minister, Atal Bihari Vajpayee, Lata Mangeshkar and Sachin Tendulkar at the Padma Awards function.

Awarded the Peace Prize by former prime minister Manmohan Singh, and Sonia Gandhi.

Receiving the Padma Bhushan from the former president, Dr A.P.J. Abdul Kalam.

Javed Akhtar presenting his book *In Other Words* to former president, Pranab Mukherjee. Also seen here, Shabana.

Lata Mangeshkar asked Javed Akhtar to release her conversational biography by Nasreen Munni Kabir. The book *Lata Mangeshkar in Her Own Voice* was published in 2009.

Amartya Sen and Amitabh Bachchan release the English translation of Javed Akhtar's book of poems, *Tarkash*. The English translation by Dr David Matthews is titled *Quiver* and was published in 2012.

(l to r) With Jagjit Singh, Pandit Shivkumar Sharma and Pandit Hariprasad Chaurasia.

With Zakir Hussain.

On his 70th birthday party in Khandala. Seen here with Shankar Mahadevan and Sonu Nigam.

With A.R. Rahman in his Chennai studio. 1999.

With Dilip Kumar and Amitabh Bachchan.

With Sridevi and Rekha.

With friend and colleague Amitabh Bachchan. The actor was voted the 'Great Star of Screen' in a millennium-celebrating poll conducted by the BBC.

Recipient of the Richard Dawkins Award for 'upholding values of Secularism and Rationalism'. Javed Akhtar is the only Asian to have received this honour.

NMK: How did he first meet Manmohan Desai?

JA: We had a meeting with Manmohan-ji on the lawns of Juhu Hotel. *Zanjeer* was about to be released and Amitabh came there to meet us. I introduced him to Man-ji:

> Manmohan-ji, this is our friend, Amitabh. He's the leading man in *Zanjeer*, which will soon be released. You'll see what great work he has done in the film.

Man-ji wished him good luck. He chatted with us and after a few minutes he left. Manmohan Desai told us later:

> You two have lost your minds. Just because you've had a few hits, you think you're messiahs and you can make anybody a star. Yeh hero banega? [You take him for hero material?]

This is a fact. That's what Man-ji said. I told him he should first see Amitabh's acting before deciding.

NMK: Did you introduce him to Yash Chopra as well?

JA: No. I don't know where they met. He was already working with Yash Chopra on a film directed by Pran Mehra, Yash-ji's former editor. That film got shelved. I think it was called *Gardish*.

The casting of *Sholay* and *Deewaar* was taking place at almost the same time. This is before *Zanjeer* hit the screens. I kept insisting that Vijay's role in *Deewaar* should be played by Amitabh. The producer, Gulshan Rai, had signed Rajesh Khanna, who was *the* star then, as he thought Rajesh Khanna should play the hero Vijay. Yash Chopra was the director and I think he might have had a bad experience with Rajesh Khanna on *Daag*. The actor must have bullied him. Yash-ji was a secretive person and used to keep his cards close to his chest, though I have a hunch he didn't want Rajesh Khanna either.

Sholay's casting was happening at the same time too. We arranged for Ramesh Sippy to see a few reels of *Zanjeer*—the whole film was still not ready. After the screening, Ramesh Sippy was convinced of Amitabh as Jai. Soon after that, Yash Chopra asked me:

Yaar, aap sab jagah iss tarah se push karte hain Amitabh Bachchan ko, yeh aapko kuchh commission de raha hai? [My friend, the way you are pushing Amitabh Bachchan everywhere, I'm wondering if he's paying you a commission.]

I smiled and said:

No commission. The fact is he's a good actor and it will benefit our film if you cast him.

We were instrumental in getting Amitabh these three films—*Zanjeer*, *Deewaar* and *Sholay*. I did most of the pushing because my conviction about his talent was so strong.

NMK: How did Jaya Bachchan get cast in *Zanjeer*?

JA: Because Amitabh and Jaya were in a relationship. Jaya was very popular and a big star, and she was choosy about her roles. Many top actresses refused the film. They didn't want to be cast opposite Amitabh, who was unsuccessful in those days. Originally, Mumtaz was supposed to play this role, though she refused too. She told Prakash Mehra:

Aap ne toh mujhe Dharmendra kaha tha, ab aap ne kisi aur ko le liya, toh mera aapka commitment khatam ho gaya. [You said you were casting Dharmendra in the lead, and you've taken someone else. My commitment is over.]

Many actresses refused. That's when Jaya offered to work in the film. When I went to see her to narrate the screenplay, she said:

Javed Sahib, aap mujhe kahaani sunaana chahte hain, zaroor suna dijiye, lekin picture toh main kar rahi hoon. [Javed Sahib, if you want to narrate the story to me, please do. In any event, I will be doing the film.] I'm doing the film for Amitabh; that's it. Do you still want to narrate the story to me?

I said:

> Phir jaane do, kaun mehnat karega! Shooting ke peheley main aapko role suna dunga. [Never mind then! Who wants to take the trouble of a narration! Before the shooting, I'll explain your role to you.]

What is ironic is the other major actors in these films, including the stars in *Sholay* and *Deewaar*, were happy we had cast Amitabh because they felt he was not much competition, and the film would be loved for their performances. They had no idea what was coming!

NMK: By 1975, with *Zanjeer*, *Deewaar* and *Sholay*, Amitabh Bachchan had flattened the competition. I think the final turning point in his career was Desai's *Amar Akbar Anthony*. How did you enjoy working with Manmohan Desai?

JA: Because of some ego hassles, which were misguided, I regret the relationship could not flourish. Manmohan Desai tried his best to be friends with us, and I think we did not respond in the way we should have. I remember he gifted a Rolex to both Salim Sahib and me. We were to blame for the relationship not continuing. Then he got disappointed with us and moved away. It was our fault.

NMK: What about your relationship with Prakash Mehra?

JA: That ended too. We worked on two films with him, starting with *Haath ki Safai*, which was in production during the shooting of *Zanjeer*. In *Haath ki Safai*, we tried to get Amitabh for Vinod Khanna's role, though somehow it did not work out because of date problems. That was the role for which Vinod Khanna got *Filmfare*'s Best Supporting Actor Award in 1975.

NMK: And Yash Chopra? You worked a lot with him.

JA: Yash-ji was very important in my life and with whom we did some key movies, including *Deewaar*, *Trishul*, *Kaala Patthar*, and then later I wrote the screenplay of *Mashaal* for him. He made me into a songwriter too.

Yash Chopra has had a long career. From 1959, when he made his first film *Dhool ka Phool,* till ... what was the film?

NMK: *Jab Tak Hai Jaan* in 2012.

JA: That's the one. He directed films from 1959 to 2012—fifty-three years! Not many directors have managed to stay relevant for as long as he did. Yash Chopra had a dip in his career for almost eight years, he was marginalised. But unlike some directors, who try to copy successful films, follow the format, Yash-ji held onto his guns and remained true to his convictions. He resurfaced and regained his place, and, as a matter of fact, came out much stronger.

He had a great sense of aesthetics. Yash-ji was drawn to the beautiful and sophisticated. His films would have a story in which the hero and heroine were real—not as real as the characters in today's films, but in those times his characters were not considered completely unreal. He had a panache for language. He cast classy actors and I can name certain heroes and heroines, however successful they were, Yash-ji would never cast because they were unsophisticated, despite all their popularity. His dialogue was well-written, the songs had good words, his music was melodious, his costumes were stylish, and his locations varied—these were his strong points. And his weak points? I don't think he was a wizard with the camera. The shot-taking in his films remained, at the most, passable. It was not very good. His editing could have been much better. I feel a certain cinematic rhythm was missing in him, though he compensated it with other important qualities.

What made him unusual and deeply impressive was the fact that he was a true leader of the team. When I talk to young directors, I always give his example. When working with Yash Chopra in any capacity, whether you were a writer, music director, set designer, or anyone, he convinced you that it was the most important film of your life. It was the one opportunity in which you could show your real talent—something you were unable to do before.

NMK: That's a major talent to have as a director, so every department wants to give their best.

JA: That's a big talent! So, actors, writers, music directors, lyricists, cameramen and editors would feel they owned the film. They believed this was the special film of their careers. Yash-ji never said: 'This is my film', 'my screenplay', my this, my that. There was no 'me' or 'I' in him. It was always 'us' and 'our film'. This is something young directors should learn when leading a team.

I believe that some of my best work was done with him. Because he had this quality to make you feel special and important.

NMK: When you narrated the story of *Deewaar*, did Yash Chopra say yes immediately?

JA: No. When we narrated the idea to him, he was rather sceptical and told us:

This has a certain resemblance to *Mother India* and *Gunga Jumna*.
I can only judge the story if you give me the complete screenplay.

Salim Sahib and I went home and in eighteen or twenty days we wrote the entire screenplay of *Deewaar*. Then we narrated it to Yash-ji and he was convinced. As I said, we also managed to convince him to take Amitabh.

NMK: Do you still meet Mr Bachchan these days?

JA: We meet at social gatherings—that's not actually meeting because we're surrounded by people and don't get a chance to talk. I am talking about spending quiet time with him. I went to his house recently and we talked for almost two hours, there was just him and me. We spoke about the old days, how writing contributes to acting, how acting contributes to writing. Being true to himself, Amitabh Bachchan said:

> Ultimately, it's the script and dialogue. What can an actor do without a good script and good dialogue?

Amitabh thinks an actor's contribution is highly exaggerated. You know how he talks about such things. I disagreed with him because you can get by with a bad or ordinary director, but films cannot afford a bad actor. A bad actor is like a wall that lets nothing pass through. I'm mortally scared of bad actors.

NMK: What about bad directors?

JA: Let's be realistic. I mean how many directors like Guru Dutt, Raj Kapoor, Vijay Anand, or Raj Khosla for that matter, do we have?

NMK: Or Mehboob Khan?

JA: Yes. How many Mehboobs or Bimal Roys have existed? These directors said something in their work, not always through words but through the language of cinema. Their camera movements spoke.

Many filmmakers in the 1970s and 1980s just filmed a script, and if the script was good and the actor performed well, the film turned out okay. Most directors relied on a good script and a good actor who would somehow compensate for the limited talents of the director.

NMK: I feel a popular film today does not use a cinematic language often enough. The films look like good TV productions and sometimes even radio plays. As you say, they depend too much on the acting or dialogue and not on the tools of cinema itself—say, using a close-up rather than words, or how and when to use background music or when to use silence.

JA: Let's not be too pessimistic! Some new-generation directors know cinematic language. Things are getting better.

NMK: As far as the political leaning of filmmakers, do you feel the directors of the 1970s were secular in their thinking?

JA: Yes, of course, they were. That was the Nehruvian India and the values remained the same for a long time. Sometimes, you see films now that are biased and have distorted values, though I think this is a passing phase.

Art can only survive if it is secular. Because it must appeal to the aesthetics of the many. Michelangelo and other artists may have made works of art about Christian mythology, but we don't appreciate those works because they are confined to Christian thought—they have transcended it and are great art, and that's why we love them. You cannot remain parochial, communal, narrow-minded in art ... that is why the right wing all over the world has been unable to create great artistes. You cannot name one great poet who is a right-winger. There is no great poet in South Africa who approved of Apartheid and wrote about the glory of racism. It is just not possible. Most writers are left of centre.

NMK: When did you start writing poetry?

JA: Sometime in 1978. I was about thirty-three. My poetry was not published then. Since I started writing at a mature age, maybe that's why I don't have many romantic poems in my collections.

In the early days, few people besides Dr Rahi Masoom Raza, Dr Harivansh Rai Bachchan, Dr Dharamvir Bharati and his wife Pushpa-ji knew that I wrote poetry. I would recite my poems to them. They were masters and learned people, so sometimes they would point out some technical mistakes I made. I learnt a lot from Dr Rahi Masoom Raza. He would say this word is right, that word is wrong, or here you're going out of meter.

NMK: Obviously, you're talking about writing poetry in Urdu. Can we speak about Urdu and its origins?

JA: Essentially, it's khari boli—a dialect spoken in western UP, and in some parts of Haryana and Delhi. Dialects are languages that are minus a script. Somewhere between 800 and 700 years ago, some people started writing khari boli in the Persian script. Because Persian was the lingua franca of the aristocracy and the upper classes at that time—not only in India but also in Central Asia. Persian had the importance and usage in its time as English does today. Even Marathi, for example, has adopted many Persian words. Take the word 'Peshwa', which means 'leader'; this is the word used for Marathi leaders—they were known as Peshwas and in many of their courts, the official language was Persian. We can see language has nothing to do with religion.

NMK: People believe that Persian was the mother tongue of the Mughals.

JA: No, the court language was Persian, but their mother tongue was Turkish. Starting from the era of Akbar, the Darbar-e-Khas was reserved for the elite and the language spoken there was Persian. Khari boli was the language of the Darbar-e-Aam—the court for common people. Khari boli is the mother of both Hindi and Urdu—we also call it 'Hindustani'.

NMK: What is your personal relationship with the Urdu language?

JA: It is my mother tongue, and I am very proud that Urdu poetry has been secular and freethinking from day one. In most other languages, we often find poetry is initially associated with religion—hymns, etc.—and later it moves onto other subjects.

The traditional Urdu ghazal, however, has been critical of religion through the use of symbols. For example, in many ghazals, preachers or saviours of the faith are seen as villains and referred to as villains—the Sheikh is the conservative, Naaseh, the counsellor/advisor, Waaiz, the preacher, Zahid, the puritan, and Muhtasib, the

man who does the moral policing. On the other hand, the hero is a
drunkard who is a freethinker or a lover whose only faith is love. Then
we have the dictionary meaning of maikhana, which is the tavern;
in poetry maikhana is a place for freethinkers. There's haram—not
haraam with a double 'a'—meaning a mosque. In the traditional
Urdu ghazal, however, haram is not a place of worship but a symbol
of conservative and regressive thinking.

NMK: Does the ghazal have its roots in Persian poetry?

JA: The ghazal belonged to Arabic literature. It has a very interesting
form that the Persians made their own and improvised on it. In Arabic
poetry, there is the qaafiya, the rhyme, but no radeef, the refrain. The
radeef are reoccurring words that come after the rhyming word. This
addition came from Persian poetry. A popular example is Ghalib's:

> Dil-e-nadaan tujhe hua kya hai
> Aakhir is dard ki dawa kya hai

'Hua' and 'dawa' are the rhyme, the radeef is 'kya hai'. Roughly
translated: 'O naïve heart, what has overcome you? What is the cure
for this affliction?'

> Koi umeed bar nahin aati
> Koi soorat nazar nahin aati

It means: 'No hope realised, no solution in sight.' 'Bar' and 'nazar'
are the rhymes and 'nahin aati' is the radeef. The qaafiya and radeef
are commonly used when writing a ghazal, whether you're writing
in Punjabi, Marathi, Gujarati or in any other Indian language.

People talk a lot about the ghazal, and it has been made very
popular by many singers. It's probably the most loved form of Urdu
poetry. But few know what a ghazal is. A few pointers may interest
people.

The first couplet in a ghazal is called a matla—the dictionary
meaning of matla is horizon—so in this context it is the horizon of

the ghazal. The matla has a qaafiya and a radeef in both lines of the couplet.

Following the matla, the first line of the ghazal's second couplet will not have a rhyme or a radeef—though it will have the same meter as the matla. However, the second line of the second couplet will have qaafiya and radeef, and the meter will remain the same.

Essentially, every couplet in a ghazal is a complete thought. That thought may or may not have anything to do with the other couplets. To me, it's like a box of assorted biscuits. You have a savoury biscuit followed by a creamy biscuit. So, each couplet can be different in thought but what strings them together is the common meter, the changing rhyme and the reoccurring radeef. Bar aati, nazar aati, dar aati and so on.

NMK: How else must one understand the ghazal?

JA: As I said, the ghazal is formed of couplets. If you are to make a statement within two lines, you will use certain symbols and metaphors. If you're familiar with Urdu poetry, you'll understand what I am alluding to when I use a symbol. Take 'rind'. The dictionary meaning is a person who drinks alcohol. In poetry it's a symbol of a freethinker.

NMK: What are the other forms of Urdu poetry?

JA: There are many. I will speak of a few.

We've talked about the ghazal, there's also the nazm that shares the same form as an English or French poem. A masnavi is a long poem that tells a complete story like Homer's *Odyssey*. The qasida is written in praise of a king, a nawab, a maharaja or someone in power. Marsiya is an elegy, and the variation of a marsiya is the noha—a lament or mourning. You have the hajva, a poem that runs someone down. The shahr ashob speaks of disruptions in society. Sauda, a contemporary of Mir, was famous for his shahr ashob.

The vasoakht is a poem from the point of view of a lover who is weary and displeased with the beloved. An example of this is Dr Qadeer's:

Tu hai harjai toh apna bhi yahi taur sahi
Tu nahin aur sahi aur nahin aur sahi

[If you are unfaithful, my stance will be the same. If not you, then someone else, if not someone else, then some other.]

I must not forget the qata [stanza]. It has four lines and has a variation called the rubaayi.

NMK: Like Omar Khayyam's *Rubaiyat*?

JA: Yes. Rubaayi is a qata in a particular meter. While qata can be in any meter, the rubaayi has a fixed meter. You have rhyming in the first, second and fourth line in a rubaayi. In qata, you're allowed to have rhyming only in the second and fourth line. Here's an example by the poet Akhtar Ansari:

Jo poochhta hai koi surkh kyun hai aaj aankhen
Toh aankhen mal ke main keheta hoon raat so na saka
Hazaar chaahun magar ye na keh sakunga kabhi
Ki raat rone ki khwaahish thi aur ro na saka

It roughly means: 'If someone asks why my eyes are red. Rubbing my eyes, I say I could not sleep last night. Much as I wished to speak, I could not speak. Last night I yearned to weep, but I could not weep.'

The following rubaayi was written by my father. As you can see it has a fixed meter with the rhyme in the first, second and fourth line:

Kyun haath jala laakh chhupaaye gori
Sakhiyon ne toh khol kar paheli rakh di
Sajan ne jo pallu tira khecha, tu ne
Jalte huye deepak pe hatheli rakh di
[Why hide your burned hand, young girl? Her friends knew the answer to the riddle. As your beloved pulled away your veil, you put out the burning lamp with your palm.]

NMK: The rules are so intricate; I'm sure you studied poetry at college.

JA: No, I learnt from listening and reading. I did not follow any course, nor did I read a 'How to write Urdu poetry' book!

I learnt poetry from some very great poets of our time who were extremely knowledgeable. If you were to recite a couplet to me, and there is a difference of half a syllable between one line and the other, I'll know it. So, when you're writing or reading Urdu poetry, your ears get so trained that you can tell the difference of even a third of a syllable. Any competent Urdu poet can figure that out.

There are of course strict rules. Unlike English poetry where you can rhyme 'time' with 'mine', in Urdu you can't—mine can only be rhymed with words like thine or shine.

NMK: Sorry, if this is a silly question, but is Sahir's *Parchhaiyan* a masnavi?

JA: That's not a silly question at all, it's a very interesting question. In fact, I have never thought about it before.

In a way, *Parchhaiyan* is a masnavi, but it does not stick to traditional rules because a masnavi is generally in one meter. Whereas Sahir has used four or five meters. I believe this is a twentieth-century phenomenon. In earlier times, one could not change the meter in a traditional masnavi, now it is accepted.

My father wrote a poem that had many meters too; it was called *Aakhri Lamha.* It was dedicated to my sister Uneza. It's a very long poem and the finest that a father could write for his daughter. He speaks of values, love, socio-political consciousness, respect for certain traditions, the courage to revolt against oppression, etc.

Let me give you an example of a traditional masnavi. This is the start of the famous *Zahr-e-Ishq* by Mirza Shauq Lakhnavi:

Rukh pe gesu hawa se hilte hain
Chaliye ab donon waqt milte hain

It means: 'A breeze blows her hair across her face. Dusk is descending, time to part.'

And this is from *Sehr-ul-Bayan* by Mir Hasan Dehlvi:

Jis mohalle mein tha hamaara ghar
Vahaan rehta tha ek saudagar

[Our house was in an area where
A merchant was once living there]

NMK: Thanks to you, my ignorance in Urdu poetry is somewhat lessening! Which of these many forms do you enjoy writing in?

JA: I'm the most comfortable writing the nazm [poem]. I have written ghazals too, but ghazals have been written so extensively by many great masters that you can feel inferior. Most of my poems are in free verse. Perhaps that is my favourite form of writing. But remember they are in free verse but are not prose poetry.

NMK: Free verse?

JA: I think it was in the 1940s/1950s that we accepted free verse, a form that came from France. Many beautiful poems have been written in free verse. Unlike traditional poetry, free verse does not have specific rules—every line need not be written in a particular meter.

We could say the difference between traditional poetry and free verse is the difference between a geet [song] and a raag. The geet will have a particular meter and be sung in it. But the raag can have alaaps of different lengths. Even while improvising, Bhimsen Joshi will sing long alaaps, short alaaps, but the scanning will remain the same and he will come back on the beat—what we call the 'sam'. For example, the beat count is 8, 16, 20, 24 or 28, but it can never be 27 or 33.

NMK: Can you tell me about prose poetry?

JA: Many people make mistakes, intentionally or unintentionally, and don't follow the inner rhythm of free verse. They try to justify their mistakes by calling it 'prose poetry'.

What is prose poetry? What is dead/alive? What is hot/cold? These are contradictions. There are clearly two forms of writing: one is prose and the other is poetry. To me, prose poetry is written by people who don't have enough control on the craft or who haven't mastered the rules of poetry. I'm totally against it.

NMK: You started writing poetry when you were thirty-three. You once mentioned you also recited your poems to Yash Chopra.

JA: Yes, Yash Chopra and his wife, Pam-ji, were among the people to whom I recited my poetry. He was a close friend, and he knew I wrote poetry.

NMK: No wonder Yash Chopra asked you to write the songs for *Silsila*.

JA: When he started the production of *Silsila*, he told me the hero was a poet, and so he wanted me to write the lyrics, but I refused. If Yash Chopra had asked any songwriter to work on his film, they'd have given their right arm to work with him. Instead, I was making some very unreasonable conditions because I didn't want to do it. To my surprise, he accepted all my conditions. I had no choice but to say yes.

When I was on my way to Yash-ji's house the next day, I was feeling a bit nervous because I was not sure I'd be able to write on the tune. I arrived there at 10.30 a.m. and met Pandit Shivkumar Sharma and Pandit Hariprasad Chaurasia for the first time. They played the tune of 'Dekha ek khwaab toh yeh silsile huey' to me. *Silsila* was a first for them and for me. When I left Yash-ji's house that evening, the tune and the words had been finalised. All in one day!

I wrote the other songs too, including 'Neela asmaan so gaya', and 'Yeh kahaan aa gaye hum'. It was my first experience and I thoroughly enjoyed it. Meanwhile, Yash Chopra's former assistant, Raman Kumar, said:

Sir, I'm making a very small film and I can't pay you what Mr Yash Chopra has paid. In fact, I can't pay you at all. But my hero is a poet too, please can you write the songs for my film?

I enjoyed writing songs so much that I agreed. So, the second film I wrote songs for was Raman Kumar's *Saath Saath,* starring Farooq Shaikh and Deepti Naval. One of the *Saath Saath* songs is still famous today, 'Tum ko dekha toh yeh khayaal aaya, zindagi dhoop tum ghana saaya [Seeing you made me think life was the noon sun and you the shade]'.

Despite my initial resistance, I thoroughly enjoyed writing songs. You write today and within a few days the song is recorded, and you are appreciated when the song has been heard by others and they say: 'Wah, wah!' You don't have to wait for two years like you do when hearing reactions to your script.

NMK: How did you like working with Jagjit Singh?

JA: My relationship with Jagjit started on a hostile note. Director Raman Kumar had chosen the composer Kuldeep Singh for the film. He's a very talented music director who also worked at the Indian People's Theatre Association (IPTA). It was decided that Jagjit Singh would sing 'Tum ko dekha toh yeh khayal aaya ...' and another song 'Pyaar mujhse jo kiya tumne toh kya paaogi [What will you gain by loving me?]'. I was very unhappy about a particular word I used in this song. I felt it had gone slightly out of meter. I thought the line had to be improved. So, Raman spoke to Jagjit to dub the line and he agreed to do it and asked us to come to a studio where he was working in the afternoon.

We arrived there on time, but there was no sign of Jagjit Singh. We kept waiting for him. He finally turned up three hours late and did not even apologise. He told Raman he had other work to finish and because he was late, he wanted to dub the line another day. I got very annoyed. I was not even charging for the film, and I only asked for a re-dub to get the best result for the song and film. I told them point blank that I would not come to the recording—it was now between Raman Kumar and Jagjit Singh. I said I didn't care anymore and walked out.

NMK: You are obviously very particular about the meter when writing a song or a poem. Can you tell me when someone could inadvertently get it wrong?

JA: For example, if you use the word 'meherbaan' in a song as a rhyming word, it will be wrong. Because the word is 'mehrbaan', not 'me-her-baan'.

NMK: But most people do say 'meherbaan'.

JA: It's wrong, just as most people say 'shukar'. There's no such word. It is shukr, zikr, fikre, lehr, shehr. The right pronounciation and correct meter are important, so one should take this into account when writing a poem or a film song.

NMK: Coming back to Jagjit Singh, did your relationship mend?

JA: For some years after the incident at the recording studio, Jagjit Singh and I did not talk to each other. If we met somewhere, we looked straight through one another. One evening at Mr Naresh Goyal's party, I happened to walk past Jagjit without looking at him. He stopped me and held my hand and said:

> Arrey chhodo, yaar. Bhool jaao vo baatein, bahut purani ho gayin. Abhi saath mein kuchh kaam vaam karte hain. [Come on, friend, whatever has happened has happened. Forget about all that now. Let us do some work together.]

I agreed that it was good to put it all behind us, as I felt his gesture was a kind of apology. So that ended that. We then made three non-film albums together, *Silsalay*, *Soz* and *Sangat*. The albums did well, but that's unsurprising because Jagjit Singh's albums were always successful. In the meantime, the *Saath Saath* song 'Tumko dekha toh yeh khayal aaya' became all the rage.

Jagjit Singh was a very unusual person. Generally, people have a pleasant demeanour when in fact they are self-centred, selfish and mean. He was brusque with people, looked uninterested, and sometimes could even be unpleasant to people, but behind all this, he hid his amazing philanthropic side. He helped so many people and institutions. I don't know why he was secretive and shy about this marvellous aspect of his personality. He was an exceptionally generous, large-hearted person, though he never let anybody know about it. I somehow heard about it through friends.

As time passed, Jagjit and I became very good friends. One evening he called me and said:

> There's a gentleman sitting in front of me, and he wants us to go to America together for some shows. You will recite your poetry and I'll sing songs from our albums. Are you free on such and such date?

I said I'd let him know the next day, and the next day I heard he had been hospitalised. That was my last conversation with him. The person who was sitting with him that evening will know what I'm talking about. I do not know his name. Jagjit's passing was very upsetting to me.

NMK: You did other non-film albums. What was your experience working with Nusrat Fateh Ali Khan?

JA: Praising him seems needless, everybody knows about his monumental talent.

I was fortunate enough to work very closely with him. He was a thorough gentleman. He had discarded every negative emotion and that purity, honesty, love and simplicity came through his singing.

NMK: How did you come to work with him on Rahul Rawail's film?

JA: At that time some music directors—I prefer not to name them—were copying Nusrat Sahib's tunes left, right and centre. So, Rahul Rawail went to London, met Nusrat and told him:

> Since everyone is copying your tunes, I prefer to ask you directly to compose music for my film ... *Aur Pyar Ho Gaya.*

Nusrat Sahib replied:

> I'd be very happy to do an Indian film, but I have two conditions. My songs must be sung by Lata-ji and Asha-ji and the lyrics must be written by Javed Akhtar. If you can manage that, I am interested.

Rahul said no problem, and that is how Nusrat Sahib came to Bombay and that's where I first met him. This was in the mid-1990s. We recorded some songs in Bombay, then he invited us to Lahore. He told me he had written a tune and had given it to a few lyricists, but they were unable to write on the tune. I asked him to play it to me. It was indeed a very difficult tune. The metering was very difficult. I said I'd try. I managed to find words to his tune, and it became the song, 'Lukchup ke main ghoomi gali gali, kahin mila nahin mera piya. [I searched in every lane; I could not find my beloved]'.

The original tune and recording by Asha Bhosle were much faster than what you can hear today on YouTube. We slowed the song down because we did not know if people could catch the words or the artistes performing the song could lip-sync it. Nusrat Sahib was very impressed and happy that the song was done. The film's soundtrack did well, and Nusrat Sahib's music was very good. By the way ... *Aur Pyar Ho Gaya* was Aishwariya Rai's first Hindi film. She was starring opposite Bobby Deol.

Like many other film soundtracks, the audio rights of ... *Aur Pyar Ho Gaya* were bought by Saregama and they asked if Nusrat Sahib and I would collaborate on a non-film album. It was later called *Sangam.* I said I'd do it on certain conditions. Nusrat Sahib is a Pakistani artiste, and I am an Indian artiste, the credit and royalty must be equal—if his picture is on the cover, mine should be too. They agreed to all our conditions and that's how it started.

The team at Saregama suggested we go to their guesthouse in Madh Island to work on the album. The guest house was beautiful, it overlooked the sea and had a big lawn where we sat and worked. Nusrat Sahib played the keyboard and sang the same line for hours, the same composition again and again. He made minor changes as if he was trying to cleanse it, make it simpler, smoother, and smoother still, and then he'd stop singing. He would look at the sea, deep in thought. He'd come back and start playing and singing again. I sat at another table and wrote. I could not help but observe him. He was free of all malice, bitterness and anger; there was nothing in him except his love for music and people. He had a good sense of humour too. It was a pleasure knowing him.

Nusrat Sahib's death was so untimely; I wish he had lived longer. The world had become his fan. He packed houses singing qawwali all around Europe and in Japan too. His audience was mainly non-Asians. He was adored. He was a kind of technical miracle in himself. Sony and other international recording companies had many plans for him. If only he had lived longer. He was on his way to America to sign some very big contracts, when he started to feel unwell, so he broke journey in London. Shabana's friend Nasreen Rehman went to meet him in hospital. He asked about me and told her to give me his salaams and said that we must meet again.

I spoke at his condolence meeting in Lahore which was held as per the tradition on the fortieth day of his passing. He was a wonderful person. There was not a negative bone in his body. He purified himself through music.

NMK: He was such a unique artiste.

JA: I still miss him a lot.

NMK: When people start off writing songs, must they have a musical background or training?

JA: No, no, though you must have a musical ear, you must have music in you. Because tunes are not always regular, they can have strange patterns and if you have a musical ear and if you can understand music, which I thankfully do, writing to a tune is easy. I know of very prominent and competent poets who came to Bombay to write songs but could not write on the tune.

NMK: When you were recording 'Dekha ek khwaab', how did you feel when you saw Lata-ji and Kishore Kumar singing your song?

JA: I couldn't have asked for more. They were my two favourite playback singers. It was like a dream come true. My first song line was sung by Kishore Kumar, so my career as lyricist started with his voice.

NMK: You have often said Kishore Kumar is your favourite male playback singer. What was your impression of him?

JA: I don't believe many people have understood Kishore Kumar despite meeting him several times. He was obviously an exceptionally talented man with a crazy sense of humour. I could tell by his conversations that when he first came to Bombay he was hurt because people did not take him seriously—they thought he had just tailed behind his brother, Ashok Kumar, who was a superstar and owner of a major studio [Bombay Talkies]. Kishore was not handsome or anything, so how could he want to act in films?

Yusuf Naqvi, the Chief Assistant in the Bombay Talkies' film *Mahal,* who knew Kishore Kumar in the early years, told me how he would sit in the studio canteen and play the tabla on the dining table. During the time he was trying to get a break as an actor or playback singer, people humiliated him. He could never get over that bitterness and hurt and was very cynical about most people. Behind his happy façade, Kishore Kumar was a lonely person.

NMK: When he and Lata-ji were recording your *Silsila* songs, did they talk to you about the lyrics?

JA: In fact, Lata-ji had a hand in my songwriting. She had a very close friend, a poetess called Padma Sachdev, a very well-respected writer in Dogri. Both she and her husband, Mr Surinder Singh Sachdev, are wonderful people. Surinder-ji is a great classical singer. They were very close friends of Dharamvir Bharati-ji and Padma-ji too. Padma-ji happened to praise my poetry to Lata Mangeshkar and so when Yash Chopra was in need of a different kind of songwriter who would introduce some freshness and a new vocabulary, Lata-ji, who was like an elder sister to Yash-ji, told him: 'You have worked with Javed as a scriptwriter, and Padma, who is such a prominent poetess herself, praises his poetry, so why don't you try him?'

I came to hear about all this much later. Yash Chopra approached me about the songs for *Silsila,* but he didn't tell me that Lata Mangeshkar had asked him to sign me on.

NMK: There was a long gap before you wrote songs for Yash-ji again. Is that right?

JA: Yes, though we were always in touch as friends. Twenty-three years, however, did pass after *Silsila*. Yash-ji called me and said he was making *Veer-Zaara* and he wanted me to write the songs. I said: 'OK, but who is the composer?' and he said: 'Madan Mohan'. I was very confused because Madan Mohan had died some twenty-eight years earlier. Yash-ji explained:

> Madan Mohan composed many tunes that were not used in any film and these tunes have been carefully preserved by his son Sanjeev Kolhi. I have asked Sanjeev to arrange and record a certain number of tunes, so you will have to write lyrics on those tunes.

So, there I was writing songs to the melodies of a music director who was no longer with us. It was so strange to hear Madan Mohan's voice on tape recorded some decades back singing the dummy words.

I have enjoyed writing songs for Yash-ji and Ashutosh Gowariker.

NMK: The *Veer-Zaara* songs and music are wonderful, and the songs remain extremely popular. And so are the songs from *Lagaan*. When it comes to screenplays, which film director do you think served them the best?

JA: Ramesh Sippy in *Sholay* and Shekhar Kapur in *Mr India*. These films could not have been better directed. *Sholay* is very good—it had superior content. On second thoughts, *Mr India* is on a par with *Sholay*. I will say only Shekhar could have directed the children in the movie as well as he did. You can't write children's innocence and spontaneity in a script; a director has to bring that out. I put *Mr India* and *Sholay* almost on the same level as far as the director's contribution is concerned. Then I like Rahul Rawail's *Betaab* and *Arjun*.

Rahul Rawail has done some great work in *Arjun*. As a matter of fact, I stumbled a little as a screenplay writer in the second half. I realised it two years after the film's release. The film was successful, it was not a flop, though it could have been remembered like *Deewaar* if the second half had been as good as the first half. I somehow missed the point, so some emotion went out of the film. It could have been a much better script with that correction. As far as the making of *Arjun* is concerned, I think Rahul Rawail was brilliant.

NMK: Do you think any of those scripts could be remade today?

JA: Obviously I would not suggest *Sholay* be remade or *Mr India*. No. They are as good as they could have been. Let's put them aside. *Arjun* could be remade with some corrections in the second half. But who will make it? I don't know, though I must say the theme of *Arjun* is about unemployment and this is still a serious problem and most relevant even today. The film also deals with how politicians manipulate situations, and that too is still relevant.

NMK: Salim Sahib and you wrote twenty-four films together and twenty were hits. I am thinking of the time when you held Meena

Kumari's *Filmfare* statuette and fantasised about winning an award—what was it like when you two won a Filmfare Award for Best Story and Best Screenplay for *Zanjeer*?

JA: Naturally, we were excited and nervous at the same time. Sweaty hands! When we were called on stage to receive the award, they only had one trophy for us. They did not know that Salim–Javed were two people. *The Times of India* editors called us to their office later to give us the second statuette. After a year, there was no such confusion. For *Deewaar,* we won all three awards: Story, Screenplay and Dialogue.

NMK: During the years that you worked together—between 1970 and 1981, eleven years—how was your personal relationship?

JA: For a long time, Salim Sahib and his wife, Salma-ji, who must be a year older than me, or maybe we're the same age, had in many ways taken the place of my missing parents, despite the fact that there was not that great a difference in our ages.

I used to call Salma-ji 'Bhabhi' [sister-in-law]. She is a wonderful lady, a kind-hearted and generous person. I have not been in touch with her in the last forty years, but that is how I remember her. And Salim Sahib was like a father figure to me. When I look back, I can see how much he influenced me for quite some time. Gradually, I realised we did not share many views; it was not my world, and I came out of the partnership. He is far more conservative than I am. He is religious and believes in certain things. For a while I was so influenced by him that I had adopted his way of thinking. But they were genuinely like substitutes for my parents, although that gradually changed.

NMK: You must have seen all their children growing up?

JA: Yes, of course. When I met Salim Sahib, Salman was less than a year old. Then the other children followed. I suggested the name for their daughter—Alvira.

Alvira was a lovely child. I will never forget an incident that happened when she was about ten months old. It was a nice day, so I carried her in my arms, and we stepped outside into the front yard. Salim Sahib's immediate neighbours was a Christian family, the Goodinos, and they had lots of chickens and little yellow chicks running about outside the house. You could hear them go 'chu-chu-chu-chu'. When I looked at Alvira, this ten-month-old child with her very big eyes—she still has big eyes—looking at those chicks, I could tell she was discovering something extraordinary. There was great surprise and curiosity on her face as she observed those chicks. Seeing this innocent curiosity nearly brought tears to my eyes. I could see this baby becoming aware of the world around her. What are these things making this 'chu-chu-chu' sound? She was like a scientist looking through a telescope and discovering a new galaxy. That was Alvira. I can never forget that moment. I was so moved by her concentration.

I genuinely wish we could retain one-hundredth of that childlike curiosity as adults. How much we might learn in life. But we lose curiosity. That is the problem.

NMK: I didn't realise you had suggested Alvira's name. How was your relationship with Salim Sahib's other children?

JA: I was very fond of Arbaaz who used to be called 'Bhai' when he was young. He was a charming and sweet child. We had a very good relationship. On the other hand, Salman was a very shy boy. He was withdrawn and reticent. He was so attached to Bhabhi. He would stand near her and seemed uneasy about going to anybody else. He was not comfortable.

All their children are good-looking because they have good-looking parents. So, it's easy for them to be good-looking.

NMK: Were they friends with Zoya and Farhan? Did they all play together?

JA: Oh yes. Salman was already a star, but whenever he saw Zoya, who was a teenager then, he'd go to the nearest shop and buy her some chocolates. He's done that many times. They still have a very good relationship. Salman treats them like siblings. I clearly remember the day Sohail was born in December 1970. That was the year Salim Sahib and I joined Sippy Films. And even now, when I see Arbaaz, he meets me with the same warmth and affection. I am very fond of him.

NMK: What does he call you?

JA: It's so sad. Arbaaz used to call me Javed uncle, but now there's such a gap between us all, so he calls me Javed Sahib. I'd prefer it if he called me Javed uncle, because Javed Sahib is too formal. But it's all right. To be honest, when I grew older, I too started calling many uncles 'Sahib'. Because after a certain age, you feel awkward calling someone 'uncle'.

NMK: Salim Sahib and you finally split in 1981, after a formidable eleven-year screenwriting partnership. Why did you stop working with one another? You have not talked much about the parting.

JA: I must tell you there were never any major fights between us. I mean, tu-tu, main-main [squabbling] happens with everyone. But serious differences? Financial or sharing of credit, etc.—no, nothing of the sort happened.

If you are partners in a cement factory, your partnership does not depend on emotions or mental rapport. You know the market rate of cement and how to split the profits. If the factory partners are decent people, all this is sorted out quite easily. Because there are clear-cut rules. The same applies to most trades.

Partners in scriptwriting—that's another ballgame. You don't know the market price of a scene; it can't be weighed or measured. How do you reach a fair conclusion? To do that you have to have a tremendous rapport between you. Because scenes aren't written in a finished form. When a scene is worked out by two people, one writer suggests something and this triggers an idea in the other writer: 'If you write that, we can add this ...'

When all the scenes are finalised, you have a screenplay. Neither writer in a partnership can claim this is your scene and that is mine. All the scenes are 'our' scenes. That's how you work. The moment that intuitive understanding and harmony goes, and the ease of communication that comes with it, you can no longer work together. In the early days when we were struggling, we were bonded together, partly because no one else bothered or cared much about us! We were a strong unit. When you become more successful, you become more relaxed, and your comfort zone starts to matter, and gradually people grow apart.

Over the years, Salim Sahib taught me many things that I can never forget. It was because of his courage I dared to ask for fees that we probably merited but I didn't believe it. He used to often tell me: 'OK, if they don't pay the fee we want, we won't work. So what!'

It was his courage and confidence that made us rise in the world of Hindi cinema. There's no doubt about that. He was far more confident than I was back then. But I'm not saying I was ever a timid person!

Sometimes parting is no one's fault, it just happens. And that's what happened to us. No sudden bitterness came between us, nor did we have a dramatic showdown. I did not say: 'This belongs to me,' nor did he say: 'No, this is mine.' We did not bicker like that. Our parting was most civilised. What made us tick as partners—that connection—had gone but the trust remained.

At that time when we parted, we had two complete screenplays minus dialogue. One was called 'Kaali' and the other 'Sailaab', both based on Salim Sahib's stories although we wrote the screenplays in tandem. As I had not written the dialogue for either project, it was not a 50/50 situation. So, Salim Sahib kept both scripts, while I took the idea of the invisible man which finally became *Mr. India*. Even though we were parting, he asked me to suggest a director and writer for 'Kaali'. I thought he should consider the director Chitrarth Singh, who made a very successful 1981 Punjabi film called *Chann Pardesi* which won a National Award. For the dialogue, I suggested Sharad Joshi, a very good Hindi writer. I know Salim Sahib trusted me and took my suggestions seriously, even though he did not know the work of either Chitrarth Singh or Sharad Joshi. He contacted both of them for 'Kaali' and Sharad Joshi even wrote a version of the dialogue, but unfortunately the film was never made.

NMK: And 'Sailaab'?

JA: I think 'Sailaab' was ultimately made with Salman with the title *Yeh Majhdhaar*. If I remember correctly, that was the only Salman movie that was released on TV and not theatrically.

What happened with 'Kaali' is beyond my understanding. Producer Mohan Kumar wanted to make it and Salim Sahib narrated the script to Rekha but, for some reason, she refused the role. I think it would have been the role of a lifetime. That reminds me—who would believe that Mumtaz refused to work in *Seeta aur Geeta*. It is difficult to understand why people come to some decisions.

A couple of years ago, I asked Salim Sahib to send me a copy of the 'Kaali' screenplay to read. I read it and felt it was outdated. It's years since we wrote the first version and since that time many dacoit-themed films like *Bandit Queen* with Seema Biswas and *Paan Singh Tomar* with Irrfan Khan changed the whole concept of the dacoit film.

NMK: *Mr. India* was released in 1987, that's almost seven years since you worked with Salim Sahib. Why did it take so long to get made?

JA: I was busy working on *Betaab*, *Mashaal*, *Arjun* and other films. As soon as I had the time, I wrote the complete screenplay of

Mr. India on my own and then the dialogue. I asked Mr Boney Kapoor, the producer of the film, to credit it as a Salim–Javed work because the genesis of the idea dated back to the Salim–Javed era— Salim Sahib and I had discussed the story together, so in all fairness I believed the screen credit should be 'Salim–Javed'.

By the time the film was released, I was well-known for my lyrics, but I asked Boney not to credit me as lyricist on the *Mr. India* posters because the posters carried the Salim–Javed name, I did not want my name to appear in any other category at least on the posters, only the credits in the film carry my name as lyricist.

NMK: What about the remake rights of, say, a film like *Deewaar*? Who owns them?

JA: Rajiv Rai, the producer Gulshan Rai's son, has all the rights, we don't.

NMK: Did you and Salim Sahib have remake rights on any of your films?

JA: In some cases, yes, like *Zanjeer*. We were originally paid 55,000 rupees, that is 27,500 rupees each, for the script. Recently, someone remade the story in Telugu without our permission, so they had to pay us a compensation of 4 crore rupees.

NMK: Do you think most creative partnerships have a shelf life?

JA: Unfortunately, they do. I think most of our work was good, but not all.

Many people still talk to me about our films, but they're talking about something we wrote forty years ago. What have we done for forty years? I don't watch my old films. I find it depressing to sit and watch films released in 1973 or whatever. It means you're living in your past. What's happened has happened. It's over.

NMK: Do you miss those years working with Salim Sahib?

JA: There's no point in missing the past because when time goes, it never comes back. Of course, I think of those days. I don't suffer from amnesia. [*both laugh*]

NMK: I suppose we all change with time.

JA: I remember how upset and hurt I was when Sagar Sahib changed my dialogue in the climax of *Sarhadi Lutera*. I laugh to myself now when I think of it. Who cares what Sheikh Mukhtar says in the climax of *Sarhadi Lutera*? Did it matter at all? At that time, the fact that Sagar Sahib had changed a few words in my dialogue made me walk out of the film. Even today, if someone changes my lines, I will walk out. Time has not made me compromise in this respect.

NMK: Going back to the 1970s, when you were starting out and had just been employed by Sippy Films, you had an intriguing encounter with Josy, a French girl. Am I right?

JA: Yes, that was another interesting story. 'Mujhe pyaas aisi pyaas lagi hai,' a song from Ramesh Sippy's *Andaz* was being filmed on Sonia Sahni, on an indoor set on one of the floors of Kamal Studio—the studio where I had spent nights sleeping in their compound. This time I was at the studio to watch the filming of a screenplay in which Salim Sahib and I were credited as additional scriptwriters. So, I saw myself as a successful young man, since I was now earning 750 rupees per month instead of 50 rupees!

In those days there were many hippies in Bombay who lived in small hotels in the Colaba area, and our extra suppliers hired some of these young foreigners to feature in party sequences. Gora [white] extras were the fashion back then and if you see the 1970s films, you'll see them sitting at tables in party scenes while a song is sung and danced by the heroine or the vamp.

Jozyann Chabel, a young French girl, had been hired as a junior artiste for this song sequence and that is where I met her. I used to call her 'Josy'. In fact, I had come across her briefly even before that day. It was during the shooting of Rajesh Khanna's film *Tyaag* at Ranjit Studio, and I had gone to meet the actor. I don't remember if *Tyaag* was ever released. I remember it was a very hot day and there was only one big fan in a corner of the Ranjit Studio set. My shirt was soaked through with perspiration, so I stood in front of the fan and Josy happened to be sitting nearby. She made some comment and we spoke for a few minutes. Lo and behold, after fifteen or twenty days, I saw her again on the sets of *Andaz*.

We started talking and she told me she was staying at the Rex-Stiffles Hotel, right behind Taj Mahal hotel. As time passed by, we met often and became very close. I used to go to the hotel to see her and she introduced me to her circle of friends. There was a lot of music and some improvised singing at their get-togethers.

Josy got attached to me, so when her friends were going back to their respective countries—they were mainly from France—she decided to stay on in Bombay. We spent every evening together, and whenever I was free in the day, I went to see her, or she came to Bandra to see me. Ultimately, she ran out of funds and was undecided about what to do. I thought our relationship was like a tunnel that had no end. That is when I told her that either we should get married—I was twenty-five and she was twenty-three or something—or she should return to France and go back to university. She was a French literature student, and I felt this situation was not right for her. She thought it over for a day or two and said it might be better if she returned home. I gave her some money in an envelope and with that she bought an economy class ticket for Paris. I went to the airport to see her off. We hugged and then she left.

When she arrived in Paris, she wrote me a letter, which I kept in my trouser pocket. Every day I thought of writing to her, but for some reason I couldn't. Some days passed and my trousers were sent to the laundry with her letter still in the pocket. I did not note her address anywhere else. Meanwhile, I had to leave the Bandra flat where I was staying, so I do not know whether she wrote to me again or not. We lost touch. Years later, in the early 1990s, Shabana and I went to Paris and went to the top of the Eiffel Tower. Standing at that height, I looked across the city and thought that Josy, with whom I had parted in 1970, must be living somewhere among the lights below. How could I find her? Maybe she was in Paris, maybe not, I didn't know.

In 2007, I was invited to inaugurate the Kala Ghoda festival in Bombay. The organisers had stuck posters up in the nearby streets, saying that the poet Javed Akhtar was inaugurating the festival—or something to that effect. The festival was taking place in a huge courtyard opposite the Jehangir Art Gallery. A stage had been erected and there were chairs everywhere. When Shabana and I entered, the audience stood up clapping.

As we were making our way through the crowd towards the podium, I heard a voice call out 'Javed'. I recognised Josy's voice immediately. She had a distinctive way of pronouncing my name—she'd say something like 'Jevaaid'. I turned around and saw her. Thirty-seven years later! There she was standing next to a French gentleman. She was wearing glasses. I went over to her and said: 'Josy?' She smiled and said: 'Yes.' I told her I had to go onto the stage and asked her to wait for me. When I was giving my speech, I added that I owed a word of thanks to the organisers because it was thanks to their invitation that I had met a friend after thirty-seven years. I told the audience that Josy and I were close friends, and she was in fact standing in the audience. Everyone stood up spontaneously and gave her a standing ovation.

Then we invited Josy and her partner for dinner and talked for hours. They said they had lived together for years and had three daughters. Josy told me she was now a professional sculptor and painter and was grateful to me for having advised her to go back to Paris. It was the right choice. She told me this was the first time in thirty-seven years that she had come to Bombay. When walking in the Kala Ghoda area, she happened to see the poster with my name on it. She was not sure it was me because in 1970, when we last met, I was not writing poetry and here advertised was 'the poet Javed Akhtar'. She figured she'd take a chance in case I happened to be the same Javed. We talked of the past and remembered many incidents. As they were leaving, I wrote down her Paris address.

A year or so later I went to Paris again and took gifts for her and her family and the man in her life. She invited me to their home, where I met her three daughters, who had heard about me from their mother. Josy said she wanted to show me something and went into the next room. A minute or two later she came back holding a frayed thirty-seven-year-old boarding card, 'Bombay to Paris' in her hand.

So that's how it is. Whenever I go to Paris, I meet her.

NMK: Had she changed a lot?

JA: We all change but we don't notice we have changed. We only see change in others. Josy is still a warm and witty person.

NMK: If you had married her, imagine how different your life would have been.

JA: Life is so random. Do you know how I got married to Honey Irani? Can you guess how?

Honey had made a guest appearance in *Kati Patang*. She was playing a spoilt seventeen-year-old girl and I could see she played it very well. Sometime later, when we were writing the screenplay of *Seeta aur Geeta* and when they were casting Manorama's spoilt daughter, I said the actor to play this character is Honey Irani. She was so irritating on the screen that she was the perfect choice for this part. Sippy Films signed her, and the shooting started in October–November 1971. Honey and I met on the sets of *Seeta aur Geeta* and on 21 March 1972, we were married.

If they had not cast Honey, supposing the dates they wanted were booked by some other producer, naturally they would've taken somebody else, and I would never have got to know her. If I had not seen *Kati Patang*, there wouldn't be a film called *Gully Boy* or *Dil Chahta Hai*. In the same way, if my father had joined Lucknow University instead of Aligarh University, he might never have met my mother.

Frankly, you don't know how things happen; you don't even know till much later that those moments led to turning points. They were key decisions. But which decision was the key decision? Getting married to Honey? Meeting her, or casting her? You don't know how your journey starts.

Things may seem random, but there are also patterns that are established. This world is like a huge pond where seven billion pipes spray out water. Each pipe sprays the water in a slightly different direction. You can imagine the multiple patterns the water creates. Throw a matchstick in the pond. You don't know where it will land. That is how life is. We are one small pipeline and a matchstick too.

What makes us humans different from other species is our capacity to think. Our minds allow us to think, to create things and record them, and this knowledge is transferred to the next generation. Other species do not have this advantage. Nights are dark, so we created electricity. If summers are hot, we have invented air-conditioners. If distances are long, we have cars and planes, etc. We solve problems. Though we still have far to go, the search for knowledge will never end. It is precisely this questioning, this curiosity, this attempt to understand things that has made us human beings; it is not faith. Faith asks you not to question and to blindly accept what exists, because everything has been created by a superior being. Some say you were destined to face a bad situation in this life because of what you might have done in your last life. To me this is absurd. It is not possible to have any kind of life after death. There is no reincarnation, hell or heaven, or Judgement Day. Death means nothingness.

NMK: You firmly believe in the here and now.

JA: Yes. The fact is we humans are conceited and we don't want to die. We want to be immortal so we have developed theories that tell us after death we will be somewhere—or we will come back again. Sorry. Death is death.

I think of my childhood and college days, those early years of struggle in Bombay when it seemed to me that I was stuck in a long dark tunnel and could not see the light at the other end. Then those unbelievable years, 1975/1976, they were made of dreams. That passed too. Our lives are made up of good and bad times—everything passes.

NMK: Your divorce too must have been tough on both of you. Why do you think your marriage to Honey Irani got into trouble?

JA: Honey is a wonderful person. When we got married, she was too young, and I was too mad. I had lived through hell from a young age, and I was quite messed up. There was so much anger, frustration, hurt and bitterness in me, and all this came out when I drank. As I told you, I was a reckless drinker.

There were many moments in those eleven years of marriage that I can never forgive myself for. I'm surprised when I think today how I could've been so insensitive. If I had been more sensible, maybe the marriage might not have gone wrong. She was inexperienced and strong, and I was mad. That's a bad combination.

The overriding credit goes to Honey that we did not let our divorce affect our relationship. It has grown into a deep friendship. We also tried our best not to let our children get affected by our separation. I know she sincerely wishes me well and I wish her well too. As time passes, I have more and more respect for her.

NMK: On the one hand you were going through a divorce, and at the same time you were seeing the release of one hit film after another. What did it make you feel seeing your names 'Salim–Javed' on the screen?

JA: Was I proud? I don't know. I'm not too sure.

You know, it's strange, and it's been like this for a long time, but I'm filled with a sense of emptiness and depression whenever I have achieved something that I have longed for. I thought success would give me great happiness, but it didn't.

That applied to everything I've achieved—whether it was buying my first house, my first car or whatever—it did not make me happy. OK, I owned it, so it's done, but what had changed? In 1977, one of our films, *Immaan Dharam*, did not do well at the box office. It did not demoralise me. I thought, OK, it didn't run. Maybe I expected more of myself. I often ask myself what do I still long for? What do I really want? These kinds of questions sometimes plague me.

NMK: Even if you don't feel satisfied by your achievements, you have many fans. Are they interested in your film work or songs, or your poetry?

JA: I have three kinds of fans. Some people like my work as a scriptwriter and lyricist, but they are not that familiar with my poetry, and those who are familiar with my poetry also like my film songs. There is a third kind of fan, maybe they know my songs and poetry, but what is more important to them is my opinion on certain subjects, what I say in interviews or on different platforms. They listen to my thoughts on history, society, rationality and the concept of nationalism. So, this third group of fans is very large, and they let it be known to me that they attend my talks and hear my speeches and discussions.

NMK: How do you deal with success?

JA: It may sound dramatic, but it's a fact that the success of my children gives me greater happiness than my own success. I feel proud of Zoya and Farhan. Honestly, I have never felt proud about my own work in the same way.

NMK: You said you feel proud of Zoya and Farhan. Were their personalities well-defined as kids?

JA: Farhan has really surprised me. Because I was extremely worried about him. I was not worried about Zoya.

Right from her childhood, Zoya was strong and precocious. Even when she was six or seven, she argued logically. Some of my friends used to call her Rani Jethmalani, the famous female lawyer of the time. She could dominate the girls and boys who were five years older than her. I was convinced she could take care of herself. She was always a leader.

On the other hand, Farhan was very quiet and shy in my presence, but in reality, he was a naughty child. One day, I found out he had told his friends some rather wild make-believe stories. There was a high building behind our bungalow, and he convinced his friends he could fly. He even told them he was attending flying school. I don't know how those children believed such a yarn because he travelled in the same school bus as they did, and by no means was he flying to school or anywhere else.

This story led to some of the children's parents complaining to Honey and I, saying they were scared their kids would try jumping off the roof terrace to see if they could fly like Farhan. I called my son and scolded him. He was seven or eight. I told him he was a liar. This was his reply:

I'm not a liar, I'm a fooler.

NMK: [*both laugh*] Did he say that in English?

JA: Yes. My children speak English all the time. In fact, Farhan learnt Hindustani by watching Amitabh Bachchan's films. Zoya did not watch many Hindi films. She used to watch Hollywood and European movies. She was very different. And that's why she doesn't have the same facility with Hindustani that Farhan has.

Farhan was gentle and shy. He was not a kid who argued and

fought. In fact, he was intimidated by Zoya. And I was worried about him. I used to think:

> Iss ladke mein dam nahin lagta hai. Iss mein resilience mujhe nahin dikhti hai. Yeh kya karega? [This boy does not have a strong will. I can't see resilience in him. What will happen to him in later life?]

But when he turned twenty-three, Farhan became a different person. I did not know, that even in his childhood, he had another persona when he was among his peer group. I came to know much later about different aspects of his personality.

Both my children have strong ideas. Their sense of values is impeccable. Sometimes, I feel they should be more pragmatic.

NMK: Do you see yourself in them?

JA: Yes, in both. Zoya and I tend to think logically and try to analyse things objectively. Farhan and I share a sense of humour, a happy-go-lucky attitude, taking things in a lighter vein, not making things into an issue. Many people have told me I could narrate a screenplay well. I think that was the latent actor in me. I may have had some acting talent that Farhan clearly has.

I must tell you about an incident. Farhan was about four or five years old, and I was lying on the bed, and he was sitting on my chest. I asked him:

When I grow old, will you look after me?

Of course.

What will you do for me?

I'll bring you cigarettes.

How will you get the money?

I'll take it from Mummy.

I give money to Mummy. If I don't earn, how will Mummy have any money?

He got very confused and thought for a while. Then he lay his head down on my chest and said:

Papa, buddhe mat hona! [Papa, don't grow old!]

I suspect by asking me to write his songs in youthful films like *Dil Chahta Hai* and *Rock On!!*, Farhan is trying to see to it that I don't grow old, or else he'll have to buy cigarettes for me. [*both laugh*]

NMK: Tell me something about Farhan and Adhuna's two daughters?

JA: My granddaughters are quite exceptional. The eldest, Shakya, is at Lancaster University where she's studying Sociology and Gender Studies. She gets 90 per cent in every exam and recently scored top marks for an article she wrote on sociology. When she was a young kid, Shakya's teachers remarked she had a huge vocabulary for her age. She writes well and is very articulate. She's cerebral and has an analytical mind. I'm sure she'll become a writer one day.

NMK: Shakya is an unusual name.

JA: Buddha was from a tribe called 'Shakya' and that is why he is called 'Shakyamuni' [the sage of the Shakyas], so my granddaughter's name means a girl from the Buddha clan.

NMK: Did you suggest her name?

JA: No, it was her parents who named her. Farhan is a great admirer of the Buddha and has a huge Buddha sculpture in his house.

My younger granddaughter is called Akira and before you ask me about her name, I will tell you it's her parents who named her. It's a Japanese name. I checked on the internet, and it can be a male or female and it means bright and clear. Maybe the inspiration was Akira Kurosawa. My granddaughter Akira is learning music. She sings very well and composes and writes her own lyrics. She wants to work in music. Recently, she has been given a seat in a prestigious music and drama school in England called Hurtwood House.

I am reminded of what my close friend Farhan Mujib's mother once told me. She said if you want to marry a girl, you must look at her mother because she will ultimately become like her mother. I say you must look at the children, and both Shakya and Akira are living proof of their mother's sense of values. Adhuna is a person with impeccable values.

I have no idea what went wrong with Farhan and Adhuna's marriage, and frankly, it's none of my business, but I'm happy that Shibani has come into our family. She is a welcome addition.

NMK: I know you're not keen on talking about your relationship with your father. But can we try?

JA: My father and I did not really live under one roof for long enough for us to form a proper relationship. So, my feelings for him were initially based on a romantic idea of how a father should be. For years, the image I had of him was shaped by my mother. She painted this idealised image of him.

NMK: Did he come to see your mother in Lucknow when she was ailing?

JA: Not often enough. He could not afford to come. You see, it's easy to blame him, but he probably did not have the money to travel from Bombay to Lucknow. He shared a room with a friend in a building called Arcadia in Byculla. He was struggling and entirely dependent on whether or not he got a film song to write. That is why he was missing in our lives. In addition, there were relatives who were insensitive and who'd say negative things about him that no kid should hear about his father.

NMK: Did he ever say he was proud of you in later life?

JA: That's not part of our culture—to praise our children directly. We let them know we're happy for them, but it's done in an indirect manner. I have never praised Zoya and Farhan in public or told them directly how I feel about them and their achievements, but they know I'm proud of them. 'Wow, you've performed a miracle, my child'—we don't say such things; we leave that to the movies. [*smiles*]

NMK: Your father died on 18 August 1976, over four decades ago, when he was only sixty-two. I wonder what you feel about him now.

JA: Death is a dividing line. The feelings you have about someone change when they die. Then you wish you had said this or that to them. The truth is if that person were still alive, your relationship would be no different. Relationships are strange things. I used to call my father 'Abbi' in my childhood. But when I turned fifteen or sixteen, I started calling call him 'Akhtar Sahib'. There was a distance between us, and this created enough space for my disappointment and bitterness to grow.

I was living in Kamal Studios when my father had his first heart attack and was admitted to hospital. I had no money and even a bus ticket was unaffordable. But I somehow managed to get to the hospital as quickly as I could. I saw him lying on the hospital bed with all those tubes around him, I could not help but go out into the empty corridor and weep sitting on the staircase. What was my relationship with this man when I couldn't think of two nice things to say about him as a father? What was upsetting me? Why was I crying? I can't explain it.

I have different feelings towards him at different times. Sometimes, I feel sad for him; at other times, I think he was a weak man. I'd like to know whether he was aware that he had let his children down. I never got the feeling he realised it. He believed it was he who was wronged in life—you can sense that in his poetry.

What makes me still feel bad is that, when I was doing well in Bombay, I should have taken care of him much more than I did. I should've put the past behind me and been there for him. I live with this feeling of guilt. From anger to guilt, from sympathy to resentment, these ghosts don't leave me.

NMK: Did you ever make peace with him?

JA: Not completely, but to a great extent, I did. I was thirty-one when he passed away. By then we were courteous to each other, although we did not discuss the past. When I was drunk, I sometimes questioned him, though he just kept quiet and didn't say anything.

NMK: Do you think you resemble your father?

JA: The idea frightens me, because I don't want to be weak like he was. Though I must confess, when I'm writing a song or a poem, I feel a particular line resembles his style. It does not happen often because we're different kinds of poets.

NMK: Were you ever curious about psychoanalysis? Did you ever ask your brother Salman about it?

JA: Salman is good at explaining things and he's a good orator. You must watch him sometime on YouTube. He's exceptional and explains complex concepts in simple, direct terms.

One day, I asked him to explain what psychoanalysis is. When he explained it to me, I told him I had come to two conclusions: one, that I needed psychoanalysis, and two, I will never go for it. I'll tell you why. Somebody asked the wonderful writer Rajinder Singh Bedi:

Bedi Sahib, you're an atheist, so why do you still have a beard and a turban and dress like a traditional Sardar. How come?

Bedi Sahib replied:

Yes, you're right. I've thought about cutting my hair and shaving my beard, but if I did that, I am afraid of the face that will emerge.

I ask myself, if I am psychologically cured, will I be still able to write dialogue, poetry and songs?

NMK: Your relationship with your brother is ever-changing. You said, sometimes you talk and at other times you stay away from contacting each other for years. But when Shabana had the accident recently, did he call?

JA: Of course. When he had some heart trouble, Shabana and I called him. Basic decency is different.

NMK: What about your father's children from his second marriage? Are you close to them?

JA: I am very close to Shahid. He's a younger brother to me. Then there are two sisters. I'm closer to the elder one, Uneza, who lives in Chicago. She's bright and intelligent and a good writer. My other sister, Albina Sharma, lives in Bombay. She is into spirituality, but then no one is perfect! I love her too and if need be, I will do anything for her.

NMK: When I hear about your relationship with your father, I am wondering whether your anger towards him worked its way into the Vijay of *Deewaar* and particularly *Trishul*?

JA: You're reminding me of an incident. The well-known Urdu writer Salma Siddiqui, who passed away in 2017, and who was married to the even more famous Krishan Chander, saw *Trishul*. We met after the screening and she said: 'Javed, I want to give you some advice. Forgive your father.'

I must disappoint you. Firstly, the scripts of *Deewaar* and *Trishul* were not created by me alone. To claim sole ownership of any character is unfair. Salim Sahib had a healthy relationship with his father and used to worship him. I never met him because he had passed away when Salim Sahib was fifteen. Though we both share the experience of losing our mothers early in life—I lost mine when I was eight and Salim Sahib lost his mother when he was eleven—*Trishul* was just a story to us. And I don't think I was writing my autobiography! [*both laugh*]

NMK: You have been working in Hindi films for over fifty years and the Hindi film industry has gone through many changes. What are the key changes you have observed?

JA: You could say we have come out of the feudal era and entered the corporate and industrial one. If you look at the directors and producers of the 1960s and 1970s, and before that era too, they were far more rooted in Indian culture and language. I'm talking about the black and white classics of the 1950s and the early 1960s where the films had a certain authenticity. The film directors were 'desi' in the way they looked at the world, while the upside today is that the current generation has a wider world vision and the downside is their roots are no longer that deep.

Let us not talk of an average Hindi film, it was bad then and is bad now. But if you see some recent films, we have improved on the form though lost out on the context.

NMK: What about the change in dialogue? It is definitely less melodramatic and closer to spoken language.

JA: You can see that flowery dialogue has mostly disappeared from Hindi cinema. Meaningful cinema is being made like Anubhav Sinha's *Article 15* and *Thappad*. I think *Thappad* is a brilliant film. There's not a single false line in the whole script. They've conveyed every emotion without indulging in rhetoric.

When it comes to good dialogue, it depends on strong characters speaking those lines. Take a film by Zoya. Her characters are not two-dimensional and very often she breaks with convention. For example, her stories don't have a villain. The father in *Dil Dhadakne Do*, played by Anil Kapoor, could have been a negative character because that's how a father in the old days was shown. He was a strict and rigid man wearing a dressing gown, standing at the top of a staircase, declaring pompously:

Ye shaadi nahin ho sakti. [This marriage cannot take place.]

The characters in old Hindi cinema rarely had grey shades and I find the characterisation is more nuanced today. That's a big step towards maturity.

NMK: Is it not regrettable how the use of the song has changed? It has almost disappeared. In earlier times, we had philosophical songs too.

JA: This is something I don't understand either—the undermining of the song. You're right, it often ends up playing in the background of a scene. Lip-sync songs are rare now.

I'm not saying every film should have songs, but some could. Sometimes, the song tells you far more than a scene. A song like 'Wo subah kabhi toh aayegi' cannot be replaced by dialogue. Impossible. It'll sound boring. But songs like these are needed by society. What about the intimate romantic song like 'Abhi na jao chhod kar'? or a melancholic song like 'Jaane vo kaise log the jinke pyaar ko pyaar mila'?

Praising nature is out. You don't often hear words like baadal, aasmaan, nadi, hawaayen, sitaare and suraj. I think the imagery of the moon has become a total no-no. I don't know why. The moon and moonlight were reoccurring images in the old songs. Also gone from the song are phool, kaliyaan, bhanware, titli, panchi. Urban life has separated us from nature.

NMK: We used to say the song was an expression of the character's inner emotions. Now, it's the voice-over that's doing that job. I think there's a link between the increased use of the voice-over and the decreased use of the song in Hindi films today.

JA: That's a good analysis. The voice-over can be an easy way out, but it does help create bridges in the narrative by informing the audience about, for example, the hero's character—this man has this kind of temperament, this is his background, etc. Instead of engaging us through scenes, which take more time—bearing in mind the audience is impatient today—the voice-over fills you in quickly. It's a narrative shortcut.

NMK: Did things start changing in India of the 1970s or was it later?

JA: The middle class of the 1970s had remnants of the mindset dating back to the 1950s and 1960s. There was a kind of 'we' back then. With the expansion of the global market and corporatisation, this 'we' has become further diluted. People are more likely to think in terms of 'I, me, myself'. Individualism might have been there earlier, but it was not something to be proud of.

NMK: What comes first, the way society thinks or the theme of a film?

JA: Oh ho! It's like asking which mirror at a barber's shop reflects the other mirror on the opposite wall [*both laugh*]. Personally, I feel society has a bigger role to play. To me, the first mirror is society, then films. At the end of the day cinema is only a reflection of society's preoccupations.

NMK: You have written many songs for films. What is the worst advice anybody has given you about songwriting?

JA: [*smiles*] Quite often, I have been asked to write a song in everyday language. For goodness' sake, there's a difference between prose and poetry, and however basic and simplified the poetry may be, it's still poetry. It's not spoken language.

NMK: When someone gave you that advice, what did you say?

JA: I told them:

> In your vocabulary a song cannot be written, only a telegram, but now even that's not possible because the era of the telegram is over.

NMK: Did they get the joke?

JA: Well, they got it, but I don't think they found it funny because the joke was at their expense. No one gives me wise advice anymore because I think people have reconciled with the idea they cannot get away with nonsense when dealing with me!

NMK: When it comes to acting styles, who do you like?

JA: Basically, I belong to the Dilip Kumar and Amitabh Bachchan era. My ideal was Dilip Kumar. My best colleague, in terms of actors, was Amitabh. I believe there was a perfect rapport and compatibility between his style of acting and my style of writing dialogue. Shall I say his performances matched the morality and the temperament of our characters? They were men who showed you the tip of an emotional iceberg and not the whole iceberg. The great skill of Amitabh and Dilip Kumar was their ability to hold back their emotions.

To me *Swades* has one of Shah Rukh Khan's finest performances because he does not play Shah Rukh Khan. He's capable of good work, especially when he's restrained and subtle. He has a natural magnetism. No one can look away when he's on the screen, so he doesn't have to do much. He could just stand and, believe me, people would not be able to take their eyes off him.

I once told him that I noticed a shot in *Darr* in which he's seen playing the drum in a Holi song and just staring longingly at the heroine. He isn't doing anything, but I can't forget the expression in his eyes. There's some strange energy in Shah Rukh. He is someone who has been dealt all four aces but throws them down too quickly.

NMK: Your stage work is a whole other aspect of your career. What made you decide to perform on the stage?

JA: Actually, I just stumbled into it. Many people asked me to write for the theatre. I refused because I know that I understand the grammar of cinema but not of the theatre. The concept of time and space is very different in both. I didn't believe I was competent to write a

stage play, and it was Mr Ramesh Talwar, a very active member of
IPTA, who asked me to create something new to commemorate Kaifi
Sahib's third death anniversary. At that time Shaukat Kaifi's *Yaad
ki Rahguzar* had been recently published. It was a lovely account
of her life with Kaifi Sahib. To Shaukat Apa's memories we added
Kaifi Sahib's life experiences—based on interviews and research. The
idea was that Shaukat Apa's and Kaifi Sahib's points of view would
come together in *Kaifi aur Main*.

The play was to start at 6 p.m. and by 4 p.m. that same day I
finished writing it. The play follows the structure of the famous
play *Love Letters* by A.R. Gurney. Shabana and I sat at two different
tables and read out the episodes of their lives. There was no time
for rehearsals, so Shabana and I went straight to the stage and read
out our parts. Kaifi Sahib's songs and ghazals were intermixed with
the narrative and these were sung by Jaswinder Singh, the son of
the composer Kuldeep Singh. Thankfully, the show went very well.
I must admit that Shabana and I had no idea it would do so well,
and that we'd find ourselves giving over 250 performances of *Kaifi
aur Main* all over the world.

NMK: What about *Tiranga* and *Raag Shayari*? They were different
kinds of shows, based on music.

JA: I wrote five poems on the Indian national flag. The poems did
not speak of the usual clichés but were about the colours of the flag
and the Ashoka Chakra. In the show *Tiranga*, I recited four poems;
each poem was about one colour of the flag. After each recitation, the
poem was interpreted musically by a world-class musician, including
Pandit Jasraj, Hariprasad Chaurasia, U. Srinivas and Zakir Hussain.
The fifth poem brought together all the musicians in a jugalbandi.
After the climax of the jugalbandi, I recited the fifth and final poem—
here all the colours come together. Obviously, the performance of
every master musician was outstanding. It was a great show. Although

I must tell you that Zakir Hussain really showed you the Ashoka Chakra through his tabla playing.

In *Raag Shayari*, I recited a poem, Shabana read the English translation, then Zakir Hussain would interpret it on the tabla. Shankar Mahadevan then sang the poetry in his own original compositions. Performing the show elsewhere became impossible to coordinate because everyone involved with *Raag Shayari* are very busy people.

NMK: You are also widely known for your work on Indian television.

JA: My first television experience was for a series about classic films of the past which was called *Rahe Na Rahe Hum* for Star Gold. Then I fronted six seasons of *Classic Legends* for Zee, these programmes centred on Indian cinema's major film practitioners. I also presented another series called *Jaane Pehchaane* for EPIC channel. It was based on stereotypical characters of Hindi cinema like the mothers, heroes, villains, vamps, etcetera, and how they have changed over time. You could say each series provided a window into the history of Indian film.

NMK: I remember seeing a poetry series you did for Tata Sky. I found it so informative.

JA: Vikram Mehra must be credited for this. He was working for Tata Sky at the time, now he's at Saregama. He's someone who thinks out of the box and one day, he said to me that we must make some shows for Tata Sky in which I'd recite dohas and Urdu couplets on different topics and explain their meanings.

I recited the wonderful dohas of Tulsidas, Meerabai, Kabir and others—dohas really are like capsules of wisdom. They have many rich layers and so does the poetry of great Urdu poets. There were some people who thought this series would not appeal to young people, but Vikram Mehra was right because, even after eight years, it can still be viewed 24/7 on one of Tata Sky's interactive services.

Over 250 performances have been held all over the world of *Kaifi aur Main*. The play is written by Javed Akhtar and read on stage with Shabana Azmi.

The album *Anant* has eight Rabindranath Tagore songs translated by Javed Akhtar into Hindustani and set to their original tunes. The songs were sung by Sangeeta Dutta and the musicians led by Soumik Datta. The live performance of *Anant* at the Victoria Memorial in Kolkata was a huge success.

With *(l to r)* Baba Azmi, Tanvi Azmi, Shaukat Azmi, Kaifi Azmi and Shabana.

With Shabana, Tanvi and Baba Azmi at an official event.

Sister of Javed's stepmother, Saeeda Apa was a great emotional support to him in his college days in Bhopal. Seen here with her daughter Baraan Ijlal, the celebrated Delhi-based artist.

With Salman Akhtar's son. Nephew Kabir is an Emmy Award winning director/editor who works in Hollywood. Kabir is now directing an American TV series.

With Salman Akhtar's daughter, Nishat. Now an illustrator, designer and creative educator, she has worked with many top American companies, including Nike. Nishat is now the VP of a US advertising agency.

Family and friends. *(back row l to r)* Anita Goyal, Shabana, Baraan Ijlal, Moonis Ijlal and Namrata Goyal. *(seated l to r)* Zoya, Farhan, Honey Irani and Naresh Goyal. Khandala.

With Uneza, Shahid and Albina *(seated in front)*. Javed Akhtar's siblings by his other mother, Khatija Talat, whom his father, Jan Nisar Akhtar, married a few years following the passing of Safia Akhtar.

With Honey Irani on the sets of *Seeta aur Geeta*, where they first met. The couple married in 1972, and later separated, but continue to remain firm friends. They have two children, Zoya and Farhan.

With Honey Irani. October 2022.

At Farhan and Shibani's wedding in February 2022. With *(l to r)* Zoya, Baba Azmi, Shabana, Farhan, Shibani, Tanvi Azmi, Honey Irani and Farah Khan. *(front row, l to r)* Shakya, Akira, Baba and Tanvi's children Meghna and Viraj. Khandala.

Agra. 2000s.

In the Paris home of the great man of letters, Victor Hugo. In Europe, Victor Hugo was the pioneering force in the fight for artists' rights. In India, Javed Akhtar spearheaded changes in the Copyright Bill for the protection of the rights of artists, and after many years of crusading, he finally succeeded in having the Amendment passed in Parliament.

NMK: Is there any doha you personally love?

JA: There are so many. I'm thinking of one in particular—it has a lot of resonance in our contemporary world. It was written in Awadhi almost five hundred years ago by Abdul Rahim, the court poet of Akbar. He also went by the name 'Rahiman' and his title was Khan-i-Khanan, which means the Khan of Khans.

> Rahiman, mushkil aa padi tere dohu kaam
> Seedhe se jag na mile ulte mile na Ram
> [Rahiman, what a dilemma. If we go straight, we will not gain the world, if we take a crooked path, we will lose Lord Ram.]

Here Lord Ram is the symbol of all the virtues and one's conscience. It basically means if you go after the material world, the spiritual will pass you by and vice versa. There's another lovely doha by Rahiman:

> Rahiman dhaaga prem ka mat todo chatkaye
> Toote se phir na jude, jude gaanth padi jaaye
> [Do not break the thread of love, if you do, it will not join again. And if does, a knot will appear.]

NMK: Beautiful imagery.

I've heard about your most recent stage show 'Main Koi Aisa Geet Gaoun'. Is the show based on your film songs?

JA: We first performed it in eight American cities three years ago. Then COVID-19 and lockdowns changed everything for two years. Now, we're travelling again in April and May 2023 to America with the show.

In 'Main Koi Aisa Geet Gaoun', I tell the back story of my hit songs. A variety of stories are attached to each song. Some are funny, some emotional and others surprising. My anecdotes are interspersed with a male and female singer and some fine musicians who perform the song. The show has two medleys as well.

NMK: What is the audience reaction? I am assuming it is made up mainly of South Asians.

JA: That's right. The audience are Hindi or Urdu speakers because the show is in Hindi/Urdu. Their reactions have been overwhelming. They love the songs, and they find it most interesting to hear about how we created those songs. In between the show itself, there's a Q&A. The audience's questions are fascinating. They show me such warmth and love.

NMK: You're so well-informed about what's happening in the world, so you must be aware of the increasing anti-Muslim feelings. Did you ever face discrimination because you're a Muslim?

JA: No. I did not give it much importance, though I knew the reason we could not buy a particular house in Juhu Vile Parle Scheme was because Shabana and I are Muslims.

That was too minor an incident in my view, and I don't hold a grudge against the people who were selling the house. I know there are people from every community and every caste, without exception, who suffer prejudice at least once in their lives, if not more often.

I was a nobody. People gave me a break and helped me to get further in films. I like to believe that I got ahead on merit. No one in the film industry discriminated against me because I have a Muslim name. Sadly, the communal temperature is increasing in society. Maybe it has not affected me directly, but if I don't personally suffer from cancer that does not mean there are no cancer patients.

NMK: What about your experience in America? Did you face discrimination at immigration, for example?

JA: It happened in St. Louis; I think it was in 1993. The Bombay bomb blast had happened and when I landed in America and went to the immigration counter, the officer there asked me to step aside. They searched my bags and questioned me for almost three hours.

There was no Google in those days, so they couldn't check my profile online. I later came to know that one of the wanted men in connection with the bomb blast was someone called Javed Chikna. At the end of the three hours, they were convinced I was not the terrorist Javed Chikna and they let me go.

NMK: In terms of the representation of Muslims in Indian cinema, in the old days we had some defined genres of Indian film, like the mythological and the Muslim Social. What do you think of the Muslim Socials? The ones made from the 1940s to 1960s?

JA: The so-called Muslim Social was as real as the Hollywood Westerns. I wonder if there ever was a one-street town in America where gunslingers met in a smoky bar and ended up duelling one another. Hollywood has created the myth and culture of gunslingers, horsemen and bandits. You never see anyone working in a 1950s Western. The cowboys are either drinking or gambling or shooting someone. At most, you'll see the hero leading a herd of buffaloes from one terrain to another. They are never seen feeding the animals, are they? It's all fiction.

In the same way, if you look at these so-called Muslim Socials—by the way, I don't know why they were called Muslim Socials, there were no Hindu Socials! Anyway, in this Muslim Social, the hero had to be a poet or a nawab. He was rarely an engineer, doctor, mechanic or businessman. The heroine was either the beautiful daughter of a nawab, who wore exquisite clothes and stood behind a chilman singing, or they were courtesans living in a kotha that looked more like a royal palace.

They may have been charming films, but they created a false world and false image. My brother Salman once went to a party in America where he met an educated Indian man who asked him:

Where are you from?

Lucknow.

A Muslim from Lucknow? Aap ke ghar mein toh roz mujra hota hoga. [You must have courtesans singing in your house every night.]

NMK: [*both laugh*] You think he got this idea from the movies?

JA: Of course! You know I spent most of my childhood in Lucknow and Aligarh and I must tell you I have never met anyone who called his or her father 'Abba huzoor'. I've only heard this in the Muslim Social.

NMK: Can you tell me how you handle relationships with people who have opposing political ideas to yours?

JA: When we speak of right-wing or left-wing people—I should be honest—I was born into a family of leftists, and yet I wanted to build my own career, make money, pursue my personal ambitions. One thing is clear—that I am a hardcore unflinching secularist. If I have any religion, it's atheism and secularism. But I do believe one should not be an extremist in one's views. You can fall into the trap of becoming as narrow-minded as a religious or communal bigot. You must try to be objective, meet people as people. You can oppose them and disagree with them on an ideological or a political basis, but there should be some room for personal relationships. A kind of apartheid in your mind is not justified.

I told you, when I was at college and in later life too, I had friends who belonged to all political hues. For instance, I knew Pramod Mahajan very well. He was a prominent member of the BJP. He has sadly passed away. I can't remember who introduced me to him, but we became good friends. Pramod-ji came from a humble background and was a self-made man. He was an exceptionally bright and helpful man. If something needed to be done in his ministry that he felt had social merit, he made sure it was done. He was fond of my poetry. I hear his daughter, who is now an MP, recited my poems on his birth anniversary.

The other BJP member I had very good relations with was Mr Arun Jaitley. I was terribly sad when he passed away. The first time I met him was when I went to see him to discuss the Amendment to the Copyright Bill—I will talk about the Bill later—but in the process we became very good friends. We never discussed politics; instead, we talked about literature, films, songs, music, cricket—he was a great cricket buff and knew so much about the game. During the time when I was a Rajya Sabha MP and attending Parliament, we had set up a routine. Every morning at about 7:30, even in winter and through the Delhi fog, I'd go to his house, and we'd have tea together. I would leave by 9:30, and Mr Jaitley then got ready to attend Parliament.

NMK: Can you tell me how the Copyright (Amendment) Bill was passed? It is such an important thing for future generations of artistes.

JA: It will take a whole book to explain to you the intricacies of how we went about getting it through. But I will try and put it in a nutshell.

The world over there is a system that when a song is played in the public domain, two royalties are generated. One is called sound recording royalty; any money earned goes to the music company or the producer who has recorded the song—the one who has spent the money recording it.

The other is called performing rights royalty, which covers the underlying music. This royalty goes to the composer and the lyricist. This is an accepted norm all over the world. There are societies, recognised by governments in different countries, that collect this money and give it to the composers and writers. Even in India, this law exists. But since this royalty is a transferrable right, the composers and writers in India were deprived of this right because of the kind of contract we were asked to sign. The producer or music company would take away all these rights from artistes—right from Pandit Ravi Shankar to a newcomer. So, anyone making an album or recording a song had to sign on the dotted line and concede performing rights. It did not take long for me to realise that no individual could stand up against the music companies and producers.

The UPA regime was in power in those days, so we prepared an application addressed to the former Prime Minister Manmohan Singh and Mrs Sonia Gandhi. The application was signed by the who's who of the Indian music industry. Our aim was to seek an Amendment to the Copyright Bill to protect the rights of composers and lyricists. Every songwriter and major composer, from A.R. Rahman to Shankar Mahadevan, every classical musician, including Pandit Shivkumar Sharma, Pandit Hariprasad Chaurasia, Ustad Amjad Ali Khan and Zakir Hussain, signed the application.

Armed with this application, I went to see Mrs Gandhi and showed her copies of the contracts that we are asked to sign. These unfair contracts stipulated that we composers and lyricists transfer performing rights not only now, but for all future technologies yet to be invented or discovered.

After Mrs Gandhi read the contract, she said: 'I wish they would be that forward-looking in other matters too.' I explained to her that the multinationals follow this practice, though not in India. In other countries, like England, Japan, France or Germany, royalties are paid to composers and lyricists. That is when her face turned red, and she said angrily:

> This is not acceptable. We'll put an end to it. I'll organise a meeting for you with the Prime Minister. Give him the details and I will also talk to Mr Kapil Sibal, who is the Minister of Human Resource Development [HRD], because Copyright laws falls under his ministry.

When I met Prime Minister Manmohan Singh, he promised to help, but told me that without the cooperation of the Opposition, and particularly the BJP, the Amendment would not pass. He advised I talk to the Opposition. I discussed the matter with the HRD minister,

Mr Kapil Sibal, whom I had met earlier. He was very enthusiastic and said he'd get it done but, like the prime minister, added I'd have to handle the Opposition because Bills proposed by Mr Sibal were often blocked by them.

The next person I met was Mr Arun Jaitley, the Leader of the Opposition in the Rajya Sabha. I was surprised that he already knew about our application. I remember him saying:

> Javed Sahib, I give you a gentleman's promise that I will see to it that my Party helps you. We will not create any problems but do meet Sushma Swaraj, the leader of the Opposition in the Lok Sabha.

I took a group of musicians and writers to Sushma-ji, who was very sympathetic to our cause. I felt on top of the world following that meeting. The Leader of the Congress, the Prime Minister of India, the HRD minister, the Opposition leaders of both Rajya Sabha and Lok Sabha, everyone said they were with us. So where was the problem? But I had no idea what I was getting into. I did not realise, from an idea to a Bill, from a Bill to an Act is more difficult than a drop falling into the ocean, finding a shell, entering it, becoming a pearl, and then being discovered.

NMK: What happened then?

JA: The idea was first presented by the HRD minister, Mr Kapil Sibal. He talked to the Secretary and the Joint Secretary, a Mr Amit Khare, and he prepared a draft of the Amendment. The draft went back and forth between the Secretary and Joint Secretary, each made their own comments. When it was approved by the HRD ministry, it was tabled in Parliament and immediately after that it was sent to the Standing Committee for review.

NMK: What is the Standing Committee?

JA: A committee made up of members of every party. It's their role to give their honest opinion on a Bill, irrespective of individual party policy. At the same time, they invite people affected by the Bill to share their point of view. So, the producers and music companies, that is, the stakeholders, were invited to present their case before the Standing Committee—these meetings were mostly held in camera. Meanwhile, the music companies, producers, and even some big stars who had turned into producers started getting very concerned and tried to use their influence to block the Amendment.

NMK: How long does the Standing Committee take to approve a Bill?

JA: There have been Bills that have been discussed for seven or eight years. When it came to our Amendment, it was sent from the Standing Committee to the Cabinet within two years. Lightning speed.

The Cabinet then added the Amendment Bill to the Rajya Sabha agenda. We were told if a Bill passes in the Rajya Sabha, it is then discussed in the Lok Sabha a few days later. And if the Lok Sabha passed it, the Bill would become an Act.

At every stage, however, a Bill can be sabotaged. There were endless hurdles. Fortunately, I knew a bureaucrat in the Standing Committee who I could ask about the progress of their report. When I called him for news, he was vague and said he didn't know any details and had not been attending office. I felt something was wrong. Why was this man being vague?

I immediately met another Standing Committee member, a Mr N.K. Singh, who is now in the BJP. At that time, he was in the JDU. He admitted that problems had been created, certain provisions in the Bill that were previously approved by the Standing Committee Secretariat had disappeared in their report. So, once again, I went to see Mrs Sonia Gandhi who spoke to Mr Oscar Fernandes, the Chairman of the Parliamentary Standing Committee. He later assured me he would sort the problem out, and he did.

On 17 May 2012, the Bill was to be presented in the Rajya Sabha. If it did not go through in the Rajya Sabha, then we'd have to wait for the next Parliamentary session, which was a few months later. We were well aware that the last date of the Lok Sabha Parliamentary session was less than a week away.

The Copyright [Amendment Bill] was about to be discussed in the Rajya Sabha when a few BJP members got up and said we should not discuss it, because there was a report about how Hindus were being mistreated in Pakistan and that matter was far more important than copyright issues. It was such a sensitive subject that one could not argue against it. I looked around, hoping to see Mr Arun Jaitley, but he was not there. Mr N.K. Singh told me Mr Jaitley was having coffee in the Central Hall, and I should call him or else the Bill would be sabotaged.

I went rushing out to find him and told him what was happening. He said calmly:

Don't worry, Javed Sahib, I will see to it that your Bill is passed today in the Rajya Sabha.

Mr Arun Jaitley finished his coffee and, along with Mr Kapil Sibal and a few other people, we made our way to see Mr Hamid Ansari, the Rajya Sabha Chairman, in his office. Mr Ansari heard the whole story, and when Mr Jaitley suggested we give his party members time to express their anger concerning the injustice inflicted on the minorities in Pakistan, and after an hour the Copyright Bill would be discussed.

I later came to know the BJP members who wanted to discuss other matters instead of the Copyright Bill were hand in glove with some of the music companies and some film stars. They were told by Mr Arun Jaitley that if they tried to sabotage the Bill, he would stand up and make a statement saying his party approves it and it would put them in a very embarrassing situation.

We all returned to the Rajya Sabha after our meeting with Mr Ansari. An hour passed, during which time the BJP members discussed other matters. The Speaker of the House then opened the discussion on the Copyright Bill. I was appointed a Rajya Sabha MP in 2010 but had not yet spoken in Parliament in those two years. When making your maiden speech you're allowed to speak for twenty minutes. I saved this privilege to present the case for us composers and lyricists when required. That day I gave my maiden speech in the Rajya Sabha.

NMK: Are you referring to your twenty-minute speech in Parliament, which is on YouTube?

JA: Yes, that's the one. By the time I started talking, it was already late in the evening. Mr Jaitley kept sitting all through that long session because he knew the moment he left, the Bill would be sabotaged by his own party members. Some still suggested discussing the Bill the next day because it was getting late. We knew that meant it could not get to the Lok Sabha in time.

I believe members of the House were impressed by my speech. After 9 p.m. that night, the Bill was passed.

NMK: But that was only half the battle. Then it had to go to Lok Sabha, right?

JA: That's right.

I came back to Bombay to attend a party at Farhan's place. There I met a very big star, I don't want to name the poor fellow, who said to me with great confidence: 'Your Bill will not pass in the Lok Sabha.' I smiled and told him we must wait and see.

The next day I rushed back to Delhi and went straight to the office of the Minister for Parliamentary Affairs, Mr Pawan Kumar Bansal, who assured me our Bill was on top of the Lok Sabha agenda—six Bills were to be presented that day. Matter finished.

I went home thinking to myself we were well on our way. Then a sympathetic bureaucrat, a Mr Raghavender, called me that evening and said: 'Javed Sahib, your Bill is not on the agenda.' I was appalled and replied:

The Minister of Parliamentary Affairs has just assured me it is. It was sent to the Lok Sabha Secretariat. You must be mistaken.

Saying that, I put the phone down and immediately called Mr Pawan Kumar Bansal who assured me once again that everything was in order. The phone rang a few minutes later. It was Sushma Swaraj:

Javed Bhai, your Amendment Bill has vanished! I know what's happening. But we'll make sure it passes. Take it easy and don't worry.

How could I possibly not worry!

NMK: What a hair-raising story! What did you do then?

JA: Shortly after speaking to Sushma-ji, I called Mrs Gandhi's Officer-on-Special Duty, Mr Dhiraj Srivastava. He said it was too late that night to see Mrs Gandhi, but proposed I write her a letter. He drafted the letter himself and came to my place for me to sign it, saying he'd make sure she would see the letter before attending Parliament the next morning. As luck would have it, my printer was not working! It really felt like a suspense movie—somehow, we got the printer going and I signed the letter.

The Minister for Parliamentary Affairs, Mr Pawan Kumar Bansal, called me back an hour or so later that same night and advised us to see Meira Kumar, the Speaker of the Lok Sabha, the next morning. At 9.30 a.m., we went to Meira-ji's office and asked why the Bill had disappeared from the agenda. She immediately called the Secretary of the Lok Sabha Secretariat, Mr Raghunath, who said one of the documents did not have Mr Kapil Sibal's signature, so it was best to postpone tabling the Bill till the next session. Meira-ji took a short pause, then she looked at me kindly and said:

Javed Bhai, you have come to me for the first time for something; we will try our best to help you. You may go and I'll talk to Mr Raghunath. We will find a solution.

Maybe Meira-ji did not wish to speak to Mr Raghnuath in my presence. A few minutes later, I entered the Lok Sabha corridor, I saw Mrs Gandhi walking towards me at great speed followed by her staff. She walks very briskly. I stood against the wall and, without stopping, she looked at me and asked: 'Is it done?' I responded: 'I don't know. Maybe.' She heard my answer as she continued walking past me.

The MP Girija Vyas then told me the Bill was indeed sent from Meira Kumar-ji's office, but who will speak in Parliament on behalf of the Congress Party? No one from the Congress was present at that time. I immediately blurted out, 'Shashi Tharoor!' Girija Vyas warned me she had just seen him leaving the building. I ran out and stopped Shashi Tharoor as he was getting into his car. I hurriedly explained to Shashi Tharoor that he must speak on our Amendment. He said: 'I don't know anything about it. I'm going home for lunch now.' I assured him:

> Don't worry, I will send a document to your house immediately. It has all the relevant information. Mr Kapil Sibal will speak first, and then Sushma-ji will address Parliament on behalf of the BJP. Please come back very soon so that you can speak after Sushma-ji has finished.

I had previously given a copy of the same document with bullet points to Sushma-ji. It outlined the salient features of the Amendment. When I went back into the Rajya Sabha, Sushma Swaraj had started her speech supporting the Amendment on behalf of the BJP. She referred to the points I had made in my notes—those notes were in a blue file lying in front of her. I can still see that blue file in my mind's eye.

Shashi Tharoor is a very smart man and he quickly read the notes I sent him and made his way back to Parliament as promised and made a brilliant speech. The Copyright [Amendment Bill] was passed in the Rajya Sabha on 17 May 2012 and in the Lok Sabha on

22 May 2012. These are historic days for us composers and lyricists. And among the proudest moments of my life.

NMK: You showed amazing single-mindedness. It has changed the fate of current and future composers and lyricists. Receiving those royalties gives some financial security to artistes. It is well-known that some great composers died in penury, at least that will not happen in the future.

JA: I only showed you the trailer! There was no end to the many ifs and buts along the way. At every turn, we thought things would go wrong. But somehow this camel got through the eye of a needle!

That is how it happened. The Amendment Bill got passed in the Rajya Sabha, thanks to Mrs Sonia Gandhi, Mr Kapil Sibal and Mr Arun Jaitley. And it was passed in the Lok Sabha, thanks to three ladies: Mrs Sonia Gandhi, Mrs Sushma Swaraj and Mrs Meira Kumar. They have protected our rights and I will always remain grateful to them for their unconditional help.

It would be totally amiss if I didn't talk to you about Ameet Datta and his family. He is a copyright lawyer who worked for over six years, guiding me through the legalities of the Copyright Bill. Even though he is an extremely busy man, he drafted official letters for me and accompanied me to meetings with various ministers and MPs. All this help was pro bono. His wife, Monica Datta, is a corporate lawyer. She, too, has helped Shabana and me for long years and refused to be paid for her work. They have a daughter called Tara. Young Tara is a very bright girl and I hope she becomes a lawyer too. Even when I am 130 years old, I'm sure I'll need a pro bono legal advisor. [*laughs*]

NMK: I wonder if pushing this Amendment through affected your own career ...

JA: [*smiles*] I was the busiest songwriter before it passed. Even today, I am paying the price. In 2005, I was recipient of all five Filmfare Awards nominations for lyrics—that was a first for any lyricist. But within two years, I did not have work as a songwriter. Some producers and music companies and a few stars hated me for pushing the Bill through. At a joint meeting they tried to dissuade me, but I told them firmly:

> Nothing doing. I am not going to back off. I'm going to make sure our Bill goes through.

NMK: So, you lost out personally once the Bill passed?

JA: Many producers boycotted me. I don't want to name them, but I did tell one producer, who was party to this boycott:

> On 4 October 1964, I came to Bombay to look for work in films, and when my father and my stepmother threw me out of the house, I had exactly 27 new paisa in my pocket. You can boycott me a hundred times over, but you cannot push me back to where I started. How bad can you make things for me? You cannot reduce my situation to the time when I only had 27 new paisa, can you? No? Well, then I'm winning.

NMK: You may think it odd, but this reminds of a story your friend Farhan Mujib told me—it's a fascinating story about something that happened when you were both at Minto Circle in Aligarh. I believe you were twelve years old.

He said there was a tree in the school yard that had a huge beehive among the leaves and branches. One day, a young boy who was standing under the tree was suddenly attacked by a swarm of bees ... remember?

JA: Oh yes, I remember! The bees had encircled him and bit him all over his face and body. The boy was screaming in agony, waving his hands about. Nobody had the guts to go near him. A teacher tried, but quickly moved back. The boy was frozen on the spot as the bees continued their attack. I was watching him from nearby and suddenly I had the presence of mind to run over to him, grab his hand, and pull him out of the circle of bees and shout, 'Run!' We both ran for our lives. The bees followed us and were hovering above our heads. I got stung too. We rushed into a classroom and shut the door behind us. The boy was in a terrible state—but I don't know why he didn't even try to run for safety and only did so when I grabbed his hand and told him to run. That's when he got the courage.

I didn't know my friend Farhan Mujib was so impressed that he remembered this story and even told it to you! You're making an interesting connection. I had never thought about it like that.

NMK: I know you're fearless in your views on many subjects. People read your comments on politics and other social issues, and they follow your Twitter posts. Do you think artistes have a duty to speak about the society they live in?

JA: The moment the word 'duty' enters the frame, it spoils everything. If you are doing things because you think you should do it, then it is not from the depth of your heart. You should treat it as your right, not your duty. You should think, I have the right to comment or write prose or poetry about the world I live in. You should say what you genuinely mean. Is it a duty? No, it's the privilege of artistes to speak out.

NMK: Do you fear controversy?

JA: It's impossible to avoid it if you have an opinion about something. There is bound to be someone or many people who have an opposite view. It's impossible that everyone will agree with you. In fact, the more passionately you express an opinion, the reaction will be just as passionate. If you speak your mind, you must be ready for controversy.

NMK: And accept it?

JA: What choice do you have? Every statement has a shadow. No matter how gently you express your opinion, it will have two sides.

NMK: Opposing an idea or opinion is different, but you are frequently abused crudely by certain people.

JA: I know. Some people try to compensate for their lack of logic by using crude words and aggressive language. You will notice something—this is true the world over—where there's a lot of poverty, whether in Latin America or certain parts of India, people eat spices. They eat green or red chillies. Why? Because the basic food is bland. To add taste, you add chillies. To me, abuse is the chilli of conversation. If the argument is not convincing, if the conversation is bland, then they try to make it effective by crude and abusive statements. I don't believe it's necessary to use bad language. I think anybody who has a little mastery over language does not need to express themselves in four-letter words.

NMK: I know you take pride in being a rationalist, but have you ever been to an astrologer or palmist out of fun? Has anything they said come true for you?

JA: I must confess, under the influence of Salim Saab, I had started believing in astrologers and palmists. But soon, the rational me rejected the idea. Though I must say, I love meeting astrologers and palmists! Not because I believe in astrology, but I want to know what these gentlemen think of me!

NMK: Do you believe in coincidence?

JA: Yes, I do. Conception and birth are coincidences in themselves.

The other day, I was thinking how the letters 's' and 'h' have played a big role in my life. My mother's name was Safia Siraj. My grandfather's name was Siraj-ul Haq. My father was called Syed Jan Nisar Akhtar. Then he dropped 'Syed' from his name. My younger brothers are Salman and Shahid. When my grandfather admitted me into school in Lucknow, he gave my name as Syed Javed Akhtar to the school authorities. The moment I admitted myself into college and could fill up my own forms, I dropped 'Syed'. In my school days, my first girlfriend's name started with an 'h'.

When I went to Bhopal, I was admitted to Saifia College and I stayed in Hilal Manzil. The first film I worked on as an assistant was *Shankar Hussain*. The first film I wrote some dialogue for, and where I met Salim Sahib, was *Sarhadi Lutera*, produced and directed by S.M. Sagar. Sippy Films played a vital role in our lives and gave us our first big break. It was during the making of our first major screenplay, *Seeta aur Geeta*, that I met and married Honey and we bought a bungalow called Sea Spring. The movies in Sippy Films that I'm associated with include *Sholay*, *Shaan* and *Sagaar*. When I parted from Honey, and a little while after I married Shabana, I moved into her flat in Sagar Samrat. Later, I bought three adjoining apartments in the same building, and Sagar Samrat has been home for the longest period in my life. Finally, I managed to build my dream house and called it Sukoon. When my first granddaughter was born, her parents chose the name Shakya for her.

Mark my words, now many young people know me as the father of Zoya and Farhan. But a day will come when I will be known as Shakya's grandfather. I hope that day comes in my lifetime.

NMK: For a man of letters, I suppose it's natural you'd think along the lines of the alphabet!

You once talked about charisma. How do you define it?

JA: I think anything that can be defined is not charisma. You only recognise charisma when it appears before you. At the same time, we humans have a kind of compulsion to find logic in everything, so let's try to find some logic together.

I believe charisma is the combination of two incompatible qualities: confidence and vulnerability. Because an average person is not a very confident person. If you are overconfident, that will irritate others and make them uncomfortable. If you lack total confidence, why should anyone admire you? There must be a combination of confidence and an expression that says: 'I can make it with a little help of my friends.' This way you don't threaten the ego or bring out the insecurities of others while being confident yourself. People will admire you without feeling inferior themselves. Charisma is an iron fist in a velvet glove.

NMK: You have charisma, Javed Sahib.

JA: Before you change your mind, let's move quickly on to the next subject!

NMK: You once said Amartya Sen, the Nobel Laureate, is among the few people whom you admire and that you considered it an honour when he quoted you in his book *The Idea of Justice*. Where did you meet him?

JA: I met him a few times in the home of my friends Poonam Muttreja, who is the Executive Director of the Population Foundation of India, and her husband, Shiva Kumar, who is an economist—in fact, many people call him Amartya Sen's Bhikshu Anand, after the name of the main disciple of Gautam Buddha.

It was in Chicago that I heard Amartya Sen talk for the first time. He is one of the most respected economists in the world. He has such clarity when he speaks, even someone like me who is unfamiliar with the jargon of economics can follow him with great ease. I believe a person who is a master of his or her subject can communicate in a language that's understood by everyone. You can only use simple language if you are crystal clear about your ideas. The clarity, sharpness and precision of Amartya Sen's mind was fabulous to witness.

NMK: Is there a subject you like talking about more than others?

JA: I do have a favourite subject and that's about the need for rationalism. Sometimes, I may be too insistent about it, but I feel people should think logically and use their reason. Because whatever is wrong in this world is in the domain of the irrational or short-sightedness.

NMK: You're the only Indian—I should say Asian—who has received the Richard Dawkins Award. The award was presented to you by Richard Dawkins himself in 2020 and is 'given to distinguished individuals who belong to the worlds of science, scholarship or entertainment, who publicly proclaim the values of secularism and rationalism ...'

JA: Yes, it is a great honour. Richard Dawkins has authored many brilliant books, including *The God Delusion*, *The Blind Watchmaker* and *The Selfish Gene*. For years he has advocated rationality, reason, logic and science. If you look at this world through the microscope of rationality and logic, faith does not stand a chance.

NMK: What is the difference between faith and belief?

JA: I believe the North Pole exists. Is it my faith? No, it's my belief. As far as the North Pole is concerned, we have evidence, proof and witnesses. Anything that can be proved cannot be called faith. Faith means accepting a conclusion without witnesses, evidence and rationale. Faith is essentially defended by emotions and feelings. So, feelings get hurt if you question it. Whereas the feelings of atheists are not hurt because they defend their ideas through reason and proof.

People sometimes ask me why I am an atheist; I have a stock answer. I am an atheist because I think. You'll be surprised when I say even the most religious person is 99 per cent an atheist.

NMK: How did you come to this conclusion?

JA: There are about ten major religions in the world. Out of ten religions, the religious man follows only one religion and regards the other religion in the same way as a rationalist does. The only time he thinks differently is when it comes to his own religion. The main difference between a religious man and us atheists is that he's rational when it comes to nine religions, and we are rational about all ten.

NMK: Faith is very important to many people, and when we talk of free speech, is it not their right to have faith or speak of it?

JA: Of course, it is their right. It's my right to believe Bill Gates is my first cousin. However, if you're my well-wisher, you'd advise I see a therapist quickly. But if ten million people become 'Bill Gaters', it will become a faith and people will have to respect the feelings and emotions connected to this faith.

I know faith is important to people. It gives them an invisible, non-existent benefactor to whom they can talk to every day. But he never talks to them, and if he did, they'd pass out with fear! Imagine a voice booming out like it did in *The Ten Commandments!*

NMK: People think of India as a religious country and not home to many atheists.

JA: It may come as a surprise to many, but India was the first country in the world where there was a movement of rationality and atheism. This movement dates to some 3,000 years ago and was called Charvaka. It was also known as the Lokayat philosophy. The founder Brhaspati and his followers rejected the idea of the afterlife and the existence of a supreme power.

NMK: Religion aside, what does your identity as a Muslim mean to you?

JA: As I said, I have no religious beliefs and despite being an atheist, I remain a Muslim. Remember, a Muslim and an Islamist are not synonyms. So, I will say I'm an atheist Muslim. Culturally, I'm a North Indian, Urdu-speaking, biryani-and-kebab-eating, nazm-writing, Urdu-literature-reading Muslim. That's my North Indian Muslim identity. No more, no less.

That said, you're not only what you think you are, but you are also what others think you are. If you're born into a Muslim family, you have a particular culture, you develop a particular taste for cuisine—your surroundings influence your aesthetics and decide the language you will speak. How can you stop being called a Muslim? The only way is by converting to another religion. You could become a Christian, Hindu, Jew, Sikh or Buddhist. But if you're a genuine atheist, you can't give up one set of what you consider 'irrational beliefs' to embrace another set of irrational beliefs. That makes no sense to me.

NMK: Do you think people have clichéd ideas of what a Muslim is?

JA: When people say Muslims are like this, or Hindus are like that, you are speaking of them as a monolith. You assume all Hindus and Muslims speak in one voice, which is just not true. Every community has all kinds of people.

NMK: Do you find Hindus and Muslims disagree with you a lot?

JA: Most do agree. Whenever I speak publicly, the audience listens to me and I'm grateful to them. But the right-wingers in both communities don't like me and they abuse me continuously and often viciously. If I criticise a Muslim fundamentalist, I get abused. If I criticise a Hindu fundamentalist, I get abused. So, I'm used to hearing abuse from both sides. Then there's the trolling—that's not debating to me, it's a release of venom.

To me, democracy can only thrive in a country when opposing views are accommodated and accepted. Traditionally and culturally, India has had room for dissension and even embraced it as essential to our pluralist polity. Any attempt to recast Indian culture into an intolerant mould must be thwarted. End of story.

NMK: I know I'm changing the subject totally—but may I ask where you met Shabana Azmi for the first time?

JA: I would not be able to tell you. If you asked me when I met Kaifi Azmi for the first time, I do not know. I have a vague memory of Kaifi Sahib's house dating back to when I was about five. Shabana was an infant then. You see, my parents and Kaifi Azmi and other literary people were members of a huge tribe called the Progressive Writers' Movement and as you can imagine everybody knew everybody. I was aware who Shabana was, although we were not friends. When she joined films in 1974, I saw *Ankur*, and found her acting most impressive, but we did not move in the same circles. We greeted one another at film events, but that was about it.

In fact, I suggested Shabana's name for a role in *Shakti*, the role that was eventually played by Smita Patil. For reasons best known to him, Salim Sahib was not in favour. Smita was my second choice. Till that point in time, she had not worked in any commercial film, and was hesitant. She feared she might get rejected by the audience if she were to act in one. I convinced Smita that she'd be fine and took her to meet Ramesh Sippy.

NMK: Were you watching many New Cinema films at the time?

JA: To be frank, I was immersed in popular cinema. I did watch New Cinema films from time to time. I saw *Sparsh* and thought Naseer and Shabana were excellent in the film. They were a great team and have given us some exceptional performances. Think of *Paar*, *Masoom* or *Khandhar*. They complemented each other.

I was particularly bowled over by Shabana's performance in *Sparsh*. I thought Sai Paranjpye's writing and direction were very good too. I also took Sai to meet G.P. Sippy and other producers, but the idea of letting a woman direct a film was alien to producers back then. During this time, Sai and I became good friends, and Shabana was a good friend of hers, so we met many times at Sai's house. Unknowingly, Sai was instrumental in bringing us together.

Shabana and I come from a similar background. We share a love for Urdu literature and poetry. We were brought together by many things—things that were no longer part of the world I was living in. All this had a magnetic quality for me.

We've been married since 1984; that's almost forty years. We cannot really be called a traditional husband and wife. What was clear from day one, and remains true even today, is that we are utterly equal in the marriage. You could describe us as friends who live together. We could have lived together without getting married, but her mother and extended family would not have felt comfortable with that idea. I don't think Kaifi Sahib would have been bothered about it.

I believe my relationship with Honey got spoilt because of my madness, and irresponsible and callous attitude. On the other hand, I cannot imagine how life would have turned out without Shabana. Before our relationship started, the breadth of my interests was very limited, and that made me uneasy. Our relationship has changed my life and broadened my horizon. Shabana has contributed immeasurably to my life and to my personality in all sorts of ways. For that I am ever thankful to her.

NMK: You must have had a terrible fright when Shabana met with a serious road accident recently. It must have been traumatic for you.

JA: It was, and for another reason too. The 17th of January [2020] was my seventy-fifth birthday, and we'd had a late night, or shall I say an early morning? We hardly slept. My cousin, Dr Sumbul Warsi, the daughter of my aunt who I called Amma, and her husband, Nawab Warsi, had not seen our Khandala house. So, I thought, since they were in Bombay, we could make a quick trip to Khandala the day after the birthday party. So, we headed off. We were four in one car, including the driver, Kishore. Shabana, who was very tired and had not slept the night before, travelled alone in the second car, so she could sleep on the backseat.

We were driving ahead of Shabana on the Bombay–Pune highway and suddenly my driver, Kishore, got a call from the other driver, saying there had been an accident and Shabana had been badly hurt.

We immediately made a U-turn on the highway and found her in her car. She was unconscious and there was blood on her face and clothes. Sumbul is a doctor, but we did not know if Shabana had a broken skull or neck or where the blood was coming from. There were some bystanders who were helpful, while others, most shockingly, were busy taking photos with their mobiles.

About fifteen minutes later, an ambulance arrived—and I'm being generous by calling it an ambulance; it was a rundown van in a terrible condition. Shabana was made to lie on something like a stretcher, it did not even have a neck rest. Sumbul and I sat in that so-called ambulance and because its shock absorbers were probably ancient, we could feel every bump in the road. Obviously, there were no paramedics.

By the time we got to the nearest hospital, which was the Mahatma Gandhi Institute of Medical Sciences, the office of the Chief Minister had very kindly left word that Shabana should be well taken care of. Mr Sharad Pawar's daughter, Supriya Sule, who is an MP, was in constant touch with the hospital staff too. The hospital doctors there took great care of Shabana. Meanwhile, I spoke to Tina Ambani, who graciously sent us a proper ambulance, and we later brought Shabana to the Kokilaben Dhirubhai Ambani Hospital in Versova. She was in the ICU for four to five days and in hospital for longer.

Thankfully, she did not have any fractures. But she suffered from severe whiplash, and her neck took over a month to recover. After some weeks of rest, she had to leave for Budapest for the filming of a Web series produced by Steven Spielberg's company.

NMK: What a traumatic day for you both.

JA: Absolutely. As I was taking her in the ambulance, it struck me that it was the 18th of January. That was the day when my mother died. Seeing Shabana lying unconscious with blood on her face and remembering what had happened on that same date in 1953 was so frightening and deeply disturbing. [*long pause*]

NMK: It is a great relief that Shabana is all right now.

Going back to the eighties, you mentioned recommending Smita Patil to Ramesh Sippy for *Shakti*. Who else have you recommended?

JA: Raj Babbar was my discovery too. My Delhi cousin, Manju, the daughter of my uncle Ansar Harwani, took me to see a play called *Nadir Shah*. Raj Babbar was the lead. I didn't know him, but he was so good that I asked him to come and meet me at the Oberoi Hotel, where I was staying in Delhi.

When I went down to the lobby to meet Raj, I immediately recognised the lady sitting next to him—it was Nadira, the daughter of Sajjad Zaheer, the founder of the Progressive Writers' Movement, and Razia Sajjad Zaheer, an important Urdu fiction writer and a very close friend of my mother's. I was so happy to see Nadira again; she was now Nadira Babbar.

I explained to Raj that we wanted him to meet Ramesh Sippy in connection with the casting of *Shakti*. Salim Sahib and I thought a new actor would be good to play Dilip Kumar's son, and because we had recommended Amjad Khan for Gabbar's role, Ramesh Sippy took our suggestions seriously. A few weeks later, the producers, Mushir–Riaz, paid for Raj to come to Bombay for the screen test. *Shakti* was a remake of the 1960 Tamil film *Thanga Padhakkam*. As usual, we made changes to the screenplay. By the way it was Sivaji Ganesan who played Dilip Kumar's role in the Tamil version.

Ramesh Sippy was in the process of considering casting Raj Babbar when Amitabh Bachchan suddenly became available. He was working on a film directed by Shakti Samanta that was also produced by Mushir–Riaz, and maybe Amitabh was unhappy with the project, so he asked Mushir–Riaz to please scrap that film and, to compensate them, he agreed to act in *Shakti*.

There was no reason under the sun to object to such a casting coup—Amitabh Bachchan and Dilip Kumar. That is how Amitabh came to work on *Shakti*. Sometime later, the man behind *Zanjeer*, the film that made Amitabh into a star, Prakash Mehra, asked me if I knew of any young actors, and I suggested Raj Babbar's name once again. Prakash Mehra liked him and gave him the lead role in *Jwalamukhi*. It's a coincidence that I happened to push both Smita and Raj into mainstream cinema.

NMK: Besides actors and singers, did you encourage any film directors?

JA: I became a great admirer of M.S. Sathyu after I saw his *Garm Hava*. I introduced him to G.P. Sippy and Mushir–Riaz. I even suggested that Sathyu direct *Shakti*. But people were not convinced, and also Sathyu himself was not very enthusiastic about the idea.

NMK: Directly or indirectly, it sounds like you have encouraged many people to achieve their potential. Do they remember you helped them once they became famous?

JA: Gratitude is the shortest-lived human emotion and that's across the world! That said, there are many people who remember.

For example, it's been almost fifty years since I fought for Amitabh Bachchan to be cast in some films because his talent was obvious to me—so even today there's mutual respect between us. We have a decent kind of relationship. I think he has some special corner, if not in his heart then in his attitude towards me.

There's also Anil Kapoor. He has been a successful actor for over three decades, and he still behaves with great humility towards me. If I want to meet him, he won't hesitate to come over that very day or the next. I pushed Shankar Mahadevan forward in the early days because I could see how gifted he was. To my embarrassment, he always mentions this to everyone he meets.

NMK: How did you meet Shankar Mahadevan?

JA: I was once writing a song for Imtiaz Dharker, and she suggested I work with Ehsaan Noorani. She said he's a very talented young man who works in a team of musicians and make jingles for ads. The appointment was fixed, and I met Ehsaan Noorani in their Bandra West studio called Purple Haze. He requested we wait a few minutes for his partner to arrive. Ten minutes later, Shankar Mahadevan came. This was my first meeting with them. I gave him the lyrics and within five minutes he made the tune and started singing the song. It was a very good tune, I loved it, and it was later recorded. A few days later, I called Ehsaan and asked if they were interested in writing film music. He said he'd talk to his partners and get back to me. He never did. Later, he admitted that he became so flustered that he didn't dare to call me back.

One day, I went to the offices of Saregama to meet Shweta Agnihotri, who is in charge of R&D, and there I met Shankar Mahadevan along with the CEO, Harish Dayani. While we were talking, I mentioned to Shankar an idea that I had been thinking about for over five years. I had even talked to different composers and singers about it. While I was in Pune once, I went to see the great classical singer Bhimsen Joshi and told him about my idea. He was amused and thought it was good. He made a paan and gave it to me. Later, his disciple told me it's a great honour if Joshi-ji makes a paan with his own hands and gives it to someone. It's an ultimate compliment. As I was leaving, Bhimsen Joshi gave me a shawl too. I was so deeply touched. He was a great singer.

Nowadays, technology allows you to edit together words seamlessly. So, the idea was to put words on an alaap. We would record the song with no pauses between words—a seamless flow of lyrics based on an alaap. Shankar is also an exponent of Carnatic music—and I asked if he'd like to work with me on it. He said he'd love to and during the same meeting, I decided the title of the album would be *Breathless*.

It took another year and half before we could complete the album because both Shankar and I were so busy. After the release of *Breathless*, I recommended Shankar–Ehsaan–Loy to directors and producers. I spoke to Yash Chopra and Karan Johar. Everyone was hesitant, saying the trio were very good at jingles, but film music was another beast. Ultimately, Karan Johar signed them up for *Kal Ho Na Ho*. In the meantime, they were composing Vidhu Vinod Chopra's *Mission Kashmir*.

NMK: You're very close to Shankar Mahadevan.

JA: He's like family to me and so is his wife Sangeeta and their children, Siddharth and Shivam. They're all very talented and are the happiest family I have ever met in my life. They share so much love, harmony and togetherness. They are a wonderful example of a happy family to me.

NMK: It's almost seventy years since your mother passed away. What does time mean to you?

JA: I can see time passing, and with age I've become more conscious that it is indeed passing. In my twenties or thirties, I did not think about it. I sometimes now ask myself—what does old age mean? I think it's your age plus ten. So, if you're fifteen, you think twenty-five is old. When you're twenty-five, you think it's thirty-five, etcetera. The age you are ceases to be old age. Now, I'm seventy-seven—it's no big deal, but eighty-seven is something else! [*both smile*]

NMK: Since that big birthday celebration in 2019, the world has changed forever with the arrival of COVID-19. How did the lockdowns in India impact on your life?

JA: The good thing was that for the first time, after some thirty-six years of marriage, Shabana and I were together for three months without any break. We spent most of the time in our house in Khandala. Sometimes, Zoya or Farhan came to stay over, or some friends visited. Honey also stayed a few days.

This house in Khandala, where you and I are now sitting, is situated in a small hill station near Bombay. It has really proved to be a great boon and help to us. Because life is simpler, calmer and secure. I named this house Sukoon, which means tranquillity. I think the peace here justifies the house's name. I find a lot of peace here. You understand what real silence is—something you miss in a big city. There is so much sound pollution in cities. I think we would have felt imprisoned during lockdown in our Juhu flat. Besides, Sukoon has a big garden where one can walk. Shabana and I talked about many things. I wrote a lot—I even finished two scripts. Now, I am in the process of selling them. I wrote some poetry. I read, though not as much as I would have liked. The OTT channels are seductive; they take you away from books. And once you fall in love with a particular Web series, it becomes addictive. I was binge-watching a lot.

NMK: Were you watching the news? Those heart-wrenching images of workers from the big cities walking miles and miles to get home.

JA: It was heartbreaking. I was depressed and deeply disturbed seeing those workers without any support or help. So many people died on their way home, so many suffered. I will never forget the image of a young girl who somehow carried her sick father back to their village miles away on a bicycle. Some people walked over a thousand kilometres to get back to their villages. I have written a poem called 'Ghar Wapsi' [Returning Home] on this great human tragedy.

I have always believed the average Indian is a good person, and it was heartening to hear that many stood on the roadside and gave people food, clothes or shoes. It was the people of India who were helping Indians. It was so touching.

NMK: Javed Sahib, if you were to give advice to your younger self today, what would it be?

JA: I'd say: Stop drinking immediately, learn another language. It could be any language—French, Bengali, Persian or Tamil. Learn a musical instrument, like a guitar or violin, or whatever. I think I've wasted at least ten years of my life. In hindsight, I could have used those years much better.

NMK: Bette Davis said something witty: 'Old age is not for wimps.' After the age of sixty, one of the main topics of discussion between friends is health issues. Do you worry about your health?

JA: No, no, I don't worry about it, but I know I should take care of it. There was a time that I would stay awake drinking till 2 a.m., and then get up the next day by 10.30 a.m. I was working, but at that age we have another energy level. I don't have that energy today, and I should make sure I don't waste the energy I have left. I should use it properly. We need to rest with age. Denying it is stupid. I'm supposed to walk for at least forty minutes a day, which I don't do. It's laziness that stops me. I used to go for walks till a few years back and then I got out of the habit, but I must get back into it.

When friends ask me: 'Why don't you go for a walk?' I tell my friends that after the second step I start feeling I'm repeating myself. And that is not expected of a creative person. [*smiles*]

NMK: Is it because you live in your mind rather than in your body?

JA: Maybe. I can probably give you many dignified excuses! But the fact is it's lethargy and laziness.

NMK: Your memory is formidable. You can recite hundreds of couplets and songs without prompts. Shabana said you have a photographic memory. And you remember your past so clearly.

JA: When I read or hear a poem, I remember it if it's a good couplet. Even if you're not a poet but have a basic sense of meter, you're compelled to remember the poem correctly. The moment you miss one word or put a word in the wrong order of the line, you'll know something is wrong. If you have a sense of meter, you cannot misremember a poem or a couplet.

Memory is related to one's interest, to a large extent. When something was happening around you, were you observing it attentively? Were you really listening when someone was talking?

Hearing is not enough. Were you interested in what was being said? If you were listening carefully, and thought about what was being said, then you'll remember. Most of time when others are talking, we are not listening, but waiting to speak.

It's like the difference between looking and seeing. Mir has written a marvellous couplet on this idea:

Sarsari tum jahaan se guzre, varna har ja jahaan deegar tha

NMK: 'Sarsari' is a beautiful word.

JA: It means cursory. 'Deegar' means another, 'varna har ja' means everywhere. The lines say: you went through life in a cursory manner, otherwise at every place there was a new world to be seen.

NMK: You have an amazing study in your Khandala house. There are thousands of books surrounding you. This home must mean a lot to you.

JA: Yes, it does. Before we moved into Sukoon, I saw the sitting room where we're talking, and I was very unhappy. Everybody said the layout was fine, the furniture was fine—so what was wrong with it? I just wasn't happy. So, I changed the whole look of the room, threw out all the furniture and bought new pieces. When it was all redone, I looked around and said to myself: 'This is the drawing room I had in mind.'

Shabana's friend Parna Patkar told us we should have a Griha Pravesh before we moved in—it's a ceremony that is performed when you move into a new home for the first time. I said: 'Fine, if you want to do it, I have no problem.'

On the day of the Griha Pravesh, we went to the Khandala market to buy some mithai. Shabana went inside the shop, and I was standing by the car. Across the road I saw two gentlemen. I recognised one of them. It was Mr Kamal Morarka, an important industrialist, who was very nice to me. He had even sponsored some of my TV programmes. Mr Morarka was very close to former Prime Minister Chandra Shekhar and was his minister at one point. Mr Morarka passed away not long ago. He was an unusually fine person.

I crossed the road, and we greeted each other warmly. He told me he too had a house in Khandala. He was very fond of houses, and I think he had a house in every big city. Then he introduced me to his friend and said:

> Meet my friend, Seksaria Sahib. He's connected with the film industry. There's a studio in Andheri in Bombay called Modern Studio. Seksaria Sahib is the owner of that studio.

My heart just froze. I knew that Modern Studio was none other than Kamal Studio. When it was leased for some years to Kamal Amrohi, it became known as Kamal Studio. I shook hands with Mr Seksaria and said I was sure he didn't know me. He said: 'Of course, I know you.' I continued:

> But you don't know, for two years I slept in the compound of your studio—in the corridors, the make-up rooms, the changing rooms, on two wooden crates under a tree, on a bench in front of the office, etc. Seksaria Sahib, I have a request. I have built a house here in Khandala and we're holding a Griha Pravesh this evening, will you please join us?

'Yes, I will,' he said. So, Mr Kamal Morarka and Mr Seksaria came to Sukoon later that day for the ceremony. That was the only time I ever saw him. It was uncanny to meet the man who was the owner of the studio where I spent months homeless, and the day I could finally build a home here in Khandala, he was one of the first guests to enter it.

NMK: I find that extraordinary. What are the chances of that happening! One in a billion. It's almost spooky. Life is strange.

JA: Yes, it can be.

NMK: What should one try to achieve in a lifetime?

JA: We can't all become Galileos and Einsteins, Shakespeares and Michelangelos, that's impossible. In our own humble way, we can make life better for ourselves and for others. At least we should not make the world a worse place than the way we entered it.

I cannot wish away tragic moments, humiliations and deprivations. I know without them, there is no life. Ultimately, we're all going to die. The fact that we were born has given us membership of a club called human society. It's a temporary membership to a club that has many facilities and comforts provided by those who were members earlier but who have left us now. And if I'm a good member, I should contribute something good too before my membership expires, or, at least, I should not spoil what is already there.

NMK: Your life is so full of ups and down, meetings and partings. Years ago, Shabana told me your favourite song was:

> Jeevan ke safar mein raahi milte hain bichhad jaane ko
> Aur de jaate hain yaadein tanhaayi mein tadpaane ko
>
> [On the journey of life, travellers meet only to part
> Leaving behind memories that sting in lonely moments]

I can see why you love this Sahir song. It fits your story perfectly. There are two versions of the song, a happy and sad version. Which one do you prefer?

JA: [*long pause*] The happy version.

NMK: We could talk forever, Javed Sahib. I'll finish with this question: What would you like your epitaph to read?

JA: Well, it could be: 'He was alive till he died.' But there won't be any epitaph.

NMK: What do you mean?

JA: You'll just have to wait for the answer.

Index

Note: Many of the events mentioned in the book date to a time when Mumbai was known as Bombay and Kolkata was known as Calcutta. For consistency, we have used the former city names.

With thanks to: S.M.M. Ausaja, Peter Chappell, Pradeep Chandra, Justin Chubb, Carrol Desouza, Shonali Gajwani, Namrata Goyal, Shameem Kabir, Priya Kumar, Soniya Panth, Safdar Shamee, Suhail Akhtar Warsi, the photographers who kindly let us include their photographs in this book, and Karthika V.K. and her team at Westland Books, including Saurabh Garge and Sonia Madan.

About the Authors

Poet, lyricist, screenwriter and social activist, JAVED AKHTAR is a man of many talents. Co-writer of many leading films of the 1970s, including *Zanjeer, Deewar* and *Sholay*, he has won countless awards, both for his screenplays and songs, across the decades. Javed Akhtar has published hugely successful collections of poetry and given lectures in various universities around the world on cinema, poetry, and rational and secular values. He is today considered a leading cultural commentator whose famous wit and insightful intellect have won him legions of fans and is the only Indian who has received the Richard Dawkins Award given to those 'who publicly proclaim the values of secularism and rationalism, upholding scientific truth wherever it may lead.' Javed Akhtar is the recipient of two of the highest civilian awards conferred by the Government of India: the Padma Shri in 1999 and the Padma Bhushan in 2007.

NASREEN MUNNI KABIR has made over 100 documentaries on Hindi cinema and written over twenty books on the subject. She enjoys translating and subtitling and has subtitled over 800 films from Hindi to English. She has been instrumental in introducing Hindi cinema to wider audiences in the UK and in Paris since the 1980s. Continuing to curate Channel 4's annual Indian film season, Nasreen has served as a governor on the board of the British Film Institute (2000–2006). Working between London and Mumbai, Nasreen has documented and archived Hindi film history through her books and TV programmes for over 40 years.